ORCHESTRATE

— YOUR —

LEGACY

ORCHESTRATE

— YOUR —

LEGACY

ADVANCED TAX &

LEGACY PLANNING STRATEGIES

BOB CROSETTO · RICK BAILEY · THOMAS BENO

Advantage®

Published by Advantage, Charleston, South Carolina.

Member of Advantage Media Group.
ADVANTAGE is a registered trademark and the Advantage colophon is a trademark of Advantage Media Group, Inc.

Printed in the United States of America.

ISBN: 978-1-59932-690-0
LCCN: 2015948000

Book design by Megan Elger.

Advantage Media Group is proud to be a part of the Tree Neutral® program. Tree Neutral offsets the number of trees consumed in the production and printing of this book by taking proactive steps such as planting trees in direct proportion to the number of trees used to print books. To learn more about Tree Neutral, please visit www.treeneutral.com. To learn more about Advantage's commitment to being a responsible steward of the environment, please visit www.advantagefamily.com/green

We'd like to thank our families, business associates and clients who encouraged and assisted us in writing this book. Our goal is to provide specific legacy planning strategies and tax solutions for the many layers of family and business finances.

TABLE OF CONTENTS

MONEY TO BURN?

In the early 1990s, my elderly father, hoping to simplify his life, wanted to give my brother and me two pieces of real estate worth about a million dollars. That would have created a tax liability for us of about $200,000 on the gain in the property's value since he acquired it.

Dad was 88 years old at the time, and we suggested that he hold on to the property and set up a trust. Upon his death, then, the property would be transferred to us with a stepped-up basis, meaning there would be no income tax on the gain in value over the years he had owned it. We would inherit the property at its current fair market value, eliminating all income tax consequences.

He didn't want to do that. So I went down to the bank, withdrew ten crisp $100 bills, and took them to Dad's house, where he was sitting in the living room. I joined him on the sofa.

"Say, Dad, do you have a match?"

"Sure, Son, here"—and he tossed me a pack. I pulled one of the bills out of my pocket, and as he watched, I struck a match. In a moment, a flame was licking at the edge of the bill.

Dad jumped to his feet. "What the hell are you doing?" he shouted. He quickly clapped his hands over the flame to snuff it out before it could do any damage to Ben Franklin's mysterious smile.

"I'm just doing what you're doing, Dad," I said. "You know— like father, like son? Except you're burning up a couple thousand of these. I have a long way to go, but I thought I'd just start with a few here tonight."

And that was all the persuasion he needed. Dad did the smart thing and spared us that $200,000 income tax bill. But he did more than that. In the years since his death, the amount he saved has had a chance to double and double again.

—Bob Crosetto

INTRODUCTION
WHAT DO YOU HAVE TO LOSE?

Each player in the orchestra pays rapt attention to the conductor. At the beckoning of his baton, the string section and the woodwinds, the brass and the percussion are ready to join in perfect harmony. Without him, the performance would fall apart in discord.

And why so? The conductor didn't write the score. Even if he is able to play any of those instruments, he is probably not the best. But he has a perspective that the musicians lack from their positions of expertise in the ensemble. The conductor understands where the whole piece needs to go. He knows how all the instruments need to blend in rhythm and tempo for best effect. He coordinates the specialists and brings in whoever is needed at just the right time.

It is a role that we certainly understand, though we are conductors of your money and legacy, not music.

In this book, we will take you on a journey—and most likely, you will find this to be uncharted territory. We have written it for the benefit of higher-earning, self-employed people who are looking for concrete ways to save for the future, protect their families, pay less in taxes, and pass on more for generations to come.

Take a look at this book's table of contents. This is a slice of America. You may not see your particular profession or pursuit among the profiles there, but you can be sure that many of those people share concerns, hopes, and frustrations similar to the ones that may have prompted you to pick up this book. In reading this book, you might decide to skip to the chapter that seems to most closely address your situation. Feel free to do so, but we suggest you then go back and read them all. In the other scenarios, you will see new perspectives on some of those same tools.

In these pages, you will find portraits of families and individuals who are facing specific challenges and who have found solutions that have helped them to move forward. Some of these portrayals are of real families that we have known. Most of them are a composite that represent true cases—that is, we have assembled the portrait out of very real elements that we have encountered. All of them are accounts of people who seem to have found eminent success, yet had trouble sleeping because they didn't know how to begin dealing with a variety of worries.

Most Americans are losing money, many times unknowingly and unnecessarily, particularly when it comes to taxes. They are paying much more than necessary, whether in income tax, estate tax or others. This is no small amount. This is a pile of money that could serve them well and grow for generations to become a family fortune, and yet they are throwing it by the basketful into the bonfire. The opportunity cost is staggering.

We can help to spare you those sad losses. In the case studies throughout this book, you will find clear examples of how we have done that for others. If their problems strike a chord with you, that is probably because in one way or another you are much like them. You have a unique set of problems, and they call for a unique set of solutions. This book is for you. In it you will learn about the most common problems of successful high achievers and the most appropriate tools that can help them.

We will describe those tools within the chapters, and you can learn much more in the appendix.

It is likely that you have advisors who you believe are taking very good care of you. Among them are probably a CPA, an attorney, and a financial advisor. However, in our experience, few people have anyone who is taking a holistic view of their situation. That's what we do. We make sure the music flows. We take an overview of your entire situation and bring new ideas to you that you can take to your various professionals. We are not here to replace any of those advisors. We are here to supplement them and coordinate an abundance of information so that you can get the results you need.

As in the orchestra, each of the professionals that are now on your team has his or her own specialty. What we are advocating in this book is a new concept: enlist a conductor to harmonize the development of your legacy.

How often do these advisors sit at the same table to discuss your situation? As your personal conductor, we coordinate a team to create your ideal legacy.

Many people are in dire need of a comprehensive and coordinated approach to tax efficiency and legacy planning. As you will see, they are looking for leverage, flexibility, and control. They need a conductor who can blend an array of instruments into a harmonious score.

CHAPTER ONE

THE REAL ESTATE DEVELOPER

In this chapter, the following solutions are discussed:

- Limited Liability Company
- Family Office
- Dynasty Trust
- Captive Insurance Company
- Life Insurance

THE SCENARIO

Mr. James Sullivan is a real estate developer who has built a successful company over the years from the ground up, to the point that it is now worth $40 million. The company has ten employees. James is 62, and his wife Nancy is 60. They have three children, one who is helping in the business and two who are not involved in it at all. They have five grandchildren. The couple is now considering how to transfer the estate as a legacy to the children and grandchildren.

THE CHALLENGES

The company has been managing with a large income tax issue each year, but currently, the Sullivans are grappling with the problem of how to reduce the estate tax that could drain away so much of their life's work.

They've been aware of the problem. They know that there is or will be a cost whether they start gifting the estate now or wait to transfer it upon their death. They know that the tax rates are high—and that with an estate of $40 million, they can't escape an estate tax bill.

As of 2015, the couple has only a $5.43 million tax exemption for each spouse, or a combined total of $10.86 million. That would still leave more than $29 million taxable, and at the top marginal estate tax rate of 40 percent, the tax bill would be at least $12 million, if not more. That's just at the federal level. If they were to add in the state transfer taxes, that bill would go considerably higher.

James and Nancy don't know what to do. They want to keep the estate intact and transfer it to their children. They just don't know how to do it.

They are also concerned about how that money will affect their children and their grandchildren and don't want them to become "trust fund babies." They want their heirs to be productive and to leave and promote a legacy of an industrious, successful family. They are aware that they could do them harm by providing too much money at the wrong time or in the wrong way. Many people spend a lifetime building their fortunes, and they know that much of their strength came from learning to deal with the hard times. How do you share the bounty with loved ones in a way that preserves their integrity? In other words, how do James and Nancy transfer their knowledge and wisdom along with the dollars?

James and Nancy are in the same position as we see many of our clients when we first meet. They don't know how to create a legacy plan so they do nothing out of fear of doing the wrong thing. When they pass away, they will be subject to whatever state and federal laws apply to their situation, and that's not a plan at all. That's a default.

People such as the Sullivans have a significant estate issue because they are, typically, land rich and cash poor. They tend to have a large liquidity problem at death. Not only do they have an estate tax looming, but they also tend to have debt that is financing their business. And so the question is this: If Nancy and James were to pass away, how would the heirs handle not only the estate tax but also the liquidity issues involving the loans encumbering the property in the estate?

In addition, if the heirs are forced to sell the real estate quickly to deal with these issues, they will likely get a reduced price on the sales. Fire sales don't bring top dollar, as everyone knows. The estate tax will be due nine months after the date of death, and prospective buyers are likely to be aware of the situation. To buy low and sell high is an age-old principle for making money. Your problem can become someone else's advantage.

If that were to happen to James and Nancy, their $40 million estate would be shrunk not only by the estate tax but also by the reduction in the value of the property itself. That is why it is critical to plan so that you don't put your estate in a situation of distress. A key concept—one you will see throughout this book— is the importance of maintaining control. You want to control what happens and not let someone else, particularly Uncle Sam, exert their control on the situation.

THE SOLUTIONS

First and foremost, James and Nancy need to have their basic estate planning documents in place. That will be either a will or revocable living trust. These documents will be the backbone for how the estate will be distributed. The will or revocable living trust provide the overall framework to the estate plan. Then, from a planning perspective, we can step back and start looking at other elements of the estate that need to be addressed to complete the legacy plan.

Setting Up an LLC

The next step in structuring James' and Nancy's legacy plan is to form a limited liability company to hold and control their significant real estate investments. This will be the largest block of assets to control in their legacy plan. We want to ensure that they will have the ability to control the LLC while they are alive and to pass it on to their heirs in an efficient manner.

The couple will be the managers of the LLC. As long as they have the mental capacity and the desire, they will be the ones to control the business decisions of that entity.

Into the LLC, they will gather all of the real estate holdings. The LLC provides the bucket that all of the assets can be transferred to. With the real estate in the LLC, James and Nancy can provide management and control over the assets. One of the nice features of the LLC is that Nancy and James, as the owners of a closely held business, can gift ownership interests in the LLC to their children and grandchildren. As with all gifts, the gifts are made at fair market value. Since James and Nancy control the LLC the gifts to the children can be discounted for lack of control and marketability because this is a closely held business.

For example, let's say that within the LLC is $10 million worth of real estate. Nancy and James have complete control of all the business decisions, so if they were to gift 10 percent of that interest to the children, that would be $1 million. However, an appraiser will look at the fair market value of that 10 percent ownership interest and allow a discount because of the non-controlling nature of that interest. If an independent appraiser determined that a 30 percent discount was applicable in this example, it would mean that fair market value is really only $700,000, reducing the size of the gift by $300,000.

The use of valuation discounts allows the gift and estate tax exemption to be leveraged in a far more efficient way. Instead of being valued dollar for dollar, the property is now transferred on a discounted basis.

The Family Office

Now that we've brought the children or grandchildren into the business, this sets up the opportunity for Nancy and James to have what is known as a family office. Instead of Nancy and James trying to talk to the children and grandchildren around the kitchen table, they are now having discussions around the boardroom table.

This gives James and Nancy an opportunity to start talking about the wisdom of making certain business decisions. Why would the family buy property A and not property B? Why would the family be putting money into this particular development?

From a business standpoint, this allows Nancy and James to talk with their children about money management. With this training, the children see a legacy instead of just a pile of money that has been passed on. Instead of having no idea how to invest the money, and perhaps blowing it, the children become intimately involved. The legacy is far more likely to continue to future generations.

Over the years, we have seen so many situations in which the founders of a business died in their 80s and had children who were in their 40s or 50s but who were incapable of managing the assets that were left to them. They were never taught how to use the money. James and Nancy struggled to build their enterprise from the ground up. They had to make the hard decisions step by step. They learned how to make the most of what they had. If the estate is transferred to the children who never had to make any such decisions, it is a plan that has been set up to fail.

Often, neither Dad nor Mom wants to give up the control that they have had so long. But there has to be a give and take, and that has been one of the biggest challenges in many of the business transitions that we have seen. The author David Bork, who has counseled hundreds of family-run businesses, writes about such issues in great detail in his book *Family Business, Risky Business: How to Make It Work.*

What you are developing through this family office arrangement is the ability to make business decisions. You are giving the next generation the tools to grow the wealth and not just let it dwindle away.

THE LITTLE RED WAGON

When my oldest son, Fred, was six years old, he had a little red wagon that he loved. We would load up his little wagon with vegetables from our family garden, and we would go down the road to visit our neighbors. Seldom did it take more than four stops before his vegetables were sold out. He got the sense of what selling was all about.

When he was 13 years old, Fred started mowing lawns. Soon he was getting more work than he could handle, so he hired two friends to do the work while he drummed up the business, took care of the bookkeeping, and made sure the customers were satisfied.

Today, he owns a multimillion-dollar business and lives in China. He has operations there, as well as in the Philippines and here in the United States. And it all started with a little red wagon full of vegetables.

How do you teach those in the next generation what they need to learn? Just get them started. As my father would often say, "The best way to learn is by doing." When a parent can find simple ways to get the children involved, it helps to build their confidence and their enthusiasm and their knowledge. It works for a six-year-old, and it works for a 40-year-old. It's only the lessons that change. The principle is the same.

—BOB CROSETTO

The Dynasty Trust

The next step for James and Nancy is to form a dynasty trust, another key strategy that complements the LLC. A dynasty trust is not a typical trust. It's an irrevocable trust that is designed to continue for multiple generations. If properly structured the assets that are held within the trust will never be subject to estate and gift taxes.

The dynasty trust can be structured to benefit your children, and if you have already left as much as you can to your children, why not start leaving assets to the grandchildren and great-grandchildren?

With the dynasty trust, as with other trust planning, you can put protections and incentives in place. Nancy and James can make clear what they expect of their legacy. They can state what is important to them, with language that sets up incentives. The trust, for example, might provide all the cost of the child's education under certain conditions, such as maintaining a certain GPA or working on a degree. Perhaps the trust is structured to encourage the heirs to go into government service, but the trust might set up a dollar-for-dollar match of the salary if an heir chooses that career to provide a better standard of living.

For a list of thought-provoking ideas on how you can tailor-make your trust and manage it from the grave, see the appendix.

Once the property and assets are in the dynasty trust, they are exempted from the future erosion from the estate tax as the trust passes through the generations. The assets will be protected until removed from the dynasty trust and placed in the child's estate. Otherwise, the assets will remain in the dynasty trust in perpetuity.

Part of the beauty of the dynasty trust is the asset protection that it puts in place. Let's say an heir wants to buy a house. If, say, $200,000 is distributed from the trust for the purchase, that amount is no longer protected. The house is at risk if the child gets divorced, gets into a car accident, or is sued. Alternatively, the house could be purchased within the trust, allowing the child to live there. Now, if there is a divorce, or an accident or a lawsuit, neither an outside creditor nor an ex-spouse can take the property. The assets inside the dynasty trust are protected from those circumstances.

By implementing the dynasty trust not only can Nancy and James say more directly that here is how they want their money to be used, but they can also put into place continuing protection for the estate. The assets would be distributed only for the purposes they wish. The bulk of the assets are protected from unknown creditors.

With a dynasty trust, it is almost as if you could put yourself in the position of saying, "If I were to live forever, how would I use my money?" If, for example, some day you had a grandchild with special needs, would you want the money to be used for that purpose? Do you want to help your heirs with their education? Even after you are gone, your directives remain in place. Whatever is important to you can be built into the trust to become an extension of your wishes. For generations hence, even from beyond the grave, you govern how the money is used and can encourage certain behaviors. You can also prohibit certain behaviors. And you can protect those assets long after you're gone—if you take the right steps.

Frankly, it's also a way to protect the heirs from their own stupid mistakes. Not only are you taking the steps to set up the LLC and teaching the next generation how to be astute at business, but now, with a dynasty trust, you are acknowledging that life can be uncertain. You are protecting the heirs from those unknowns down the road. You are encouraging appropriate behaviors and discouraging those that may harm your legacy.

You could even structure the trust so that every year, perhaps at Christmas or on a birthday, each of the heirs would get $500 from Grandpa and Grandma—even decades after Grandpa and Grandma last walked the earth. It's a way to keep the memories and the legacy alive. You can be sure that those in the family would know who their great-grandfather was if they're still getting benefits from his trust. A legacy can be multigenerational. In the trust, you tell those future generations, "This is who I was, this is what I believed, and this is what I wanted as a way to protect the future for all of us."

Money is meaningless except for what it represents. It gives you choices and options that you might not have otherwise. It represents all of your hard work and your years of wisdom and experience. You want to pass that on, as well, for the benefit of generations to come.

Think of it this way: If you were to live for 500 more years, what would be your concerns? Think of what you care about and how that might look in the future. Based on that, you will write the instructions for the dynasty trust. The dynasty trust is for those who can look ahead more than one or two generations and say, "If my money were to last that long, what would I want to encourage, and what would I want to discourage?"

The Captive Insurance Company

Any type of an operating business will face risks. In the case of a real estate developer, those risks are significant, whether they involve his new construction projects or those already built.

For a lot of those risks, he can simply buy readily available, commercial insurance. Most companies can purchase a general liability policy. Companies with employees can purchase workers' compensation coverage. Professionals can purchase malpractice insurance. Business owners are willing to bear the cost of those insurances because they know that the coverage protects them from events that, were they to occur, could destroy them financially.

However, other risks also come into play. For example, a real estate developer might offer warranties against defects in the workmanship on his properties. Other risks may be environmental damage or breach of a client's personal information. Typically, those are the types of risks that the business owner takes upon himself or herself, figuring it's just part of the cost of doing business. Still, those risks can be significant.

To cover these other risks, business owners are allowed to set up what are called captive insurance companies or captive reinsurance companies. Basically, the business owner can set up their own small insurance company to cover themselves. In essence, they are setting money aside in case those risks were to occur. They are considered "captive" in that the policyholder actually owns the company, which exists for the policyholder's purposes.

The business owner then pays premiums to that captive insurance company—and those premiums, up to $1.2 million per year, are tax deductible for the business, and they are not taxable to the captive insurance company.

Let's say the Sullivans were to set up such a captive insurance company. They could have the dynasty trust own it. Now, let's say the premium is $1 million a year. That money is there to pay for any risks that might occur. However, if the risks do not occur, $1 million has been transferred from the operating business into the captive insurance company. Since the captive insurance company is inside the dynasty trust, in effect, the Sullivans have now moved money to the next generation without any gift tax or estate tax. The dynasty trust would be responsible for any income tax generated by the captive insurance company.

But that's not all—because that money has been set aside for premiums, it has been spared at least 40 percent in income taxes. And so, instead of transferring $600,000, the developer was able to move $1 million. That represents an opportunity cost of $400,000.

The captive insurance company is certainly a great tool for the right situation—and this is one of them. A business owner can insure against additional risks, and, if those risks don't occur, enjoy the profits through the captive insurance company.

As with all the planning tools we discuss in this book, the captive insurance company works for some people, in some situations, just as the dynasty trust works for some people in some situations. It's like having a quiver full of arrows, with each arrow designed for a particular target.

Life Insurance

Life insurance is another one of those arrows. It isn't the perfect solution for everybody but often provides the leverage and solves a financial problem in a way that is not possible with any other tool.

For James and Nancy, life insurance plays a significant role. Real estate developers, typically, are land rich and cash poor. They often do a great job managing income taxes, but the estate tax bill becomes an ever growing issue. The goal when implementing the legacy plan is to start reducing the size of the estate over time.

However, in the case of a large estate, whatever amount is above the estate tax exemption is currently subject to a top marginal estate tax rate of 40 percent. We know that there is a large bill coming that needs to be addressed.

Through life insurance, we have the opportunity to, basically, pay the estate tax bill on discounted dollars. More importantly, it's going to provide liquidity to the estate. That way, the heirs have the money to pay the tax bill when it is needed, rather than being forced to sell the property in what might be a down market or at a fire-sale price.

In this case, since James and Nancy have a dynasty trust in place, we most likely would recommend that the life insurance be owned inside the dynasty trust so that it is outside of the estate. In this manner, the life insurance will provide liquidity to pay the estate tax, while not being includable in the estate itself. It can also give the heirs the liquidity that they need to pay off any loans due on the properties if need be—for example, the bank may call the loan upon the borrower's death.

The heirs, then, are able to keep the legacy property in place, and with the life insurance, they are paying perhaps ten cents on the dollar compared to the cost of the estate tax. In other words, if there were an estate tax of $10 million, the cost of the life insurance might be a million. This creates $9 million of leverage. How many properties would the heirs have had to sell to get that same $10 million in a fire-sale situation?

Life insurance is always a tool to consider, but of course, it will depend upon the financial situation and, as in this case, whether Nancy or James or both are insurable. The circumstances will determine whether it's a good fit, but in many cases it's a great solution. The heirs pay no income tax on the life insurance benefit, and it provides that powerful leverage. And again, because it's inside the trust, it's outside the estate, and therefore the benefit is protected from the estate tax, as well.

People get confused about the tax benefits of life insurance. They hear life insurance is tax-free. Life insurance is usually income tax-free, but if you are the owner or beneficiary of your policy it is treated as part of your estate. So in this case, let's say Nancy and James owned a $10 million policy, and it paid to their estate. After being subjected to the 40 percent marginal tax, that payout shrinks to $6 million. Uncle Sam wants his cut. But if we put that policy, from day one, inside the trust, it's outside the estate. The $10 million is free of income and estate tax.

It's one of the fundamentals of how insurance and estate taxes work, and yet it is not widely known. Knowing both what the tax implications are, and how to legally navigate them, can provide a great sense of relief and benefit.

HOW IT ALL TURNED OUT

Through careful planning, the Sullivans were able to treat all of their children fairly—those who were in the business and those who were not. They were able to groom the next generation to participate responsibly in the family's financial affairs.

In setting up the limited liability company, James and Nancy made an initial gift in the amount of half the estate exemption using the LLC membership interests. James and Nancy saved on taxes by taking advantage of the valuation discount for the gift. Then James and Nancy also set up an annual gifting plan so that they could start moving more of the LLC interest to the children each year, using the annual gift tax exclusion.

James and Nancy purchased a $10 million second-to-die life insurance policy to provide the liquidity that would be needed at the time of the surviving spouse's death to cover estate taxes. They also set up an annual valuation plan in order to determine whether additional insurance will be needed.

By establishing the dynasty trust, they were able to include incentive language reflecting their desires for the family. In addition, they began operating the LLC as a family office, in which they could teach the children about the wisdom of purchasing, or not purchasing, certain assets. This wisdom will play a large role in allowing the real estate development company to continue through future generations.

THE NEEDS, THE FEARS, THE HOPES

The prospective client and I had been chatting for the better part of an hour. After a while, when there was a pause in the conversation, I offered a few of my observations.

"Let me tell you a few things that it looks as if we would want to incorporate into your legacy plan," I said.

She raised her eyebrows and looked a bit surprised, even upset. "How could you possibly know what would be best yet?" she asked. "I'd think you would want to ask me some questions and find out something about me and my situation."

"Well," I said, "I can tell you how many children you have, their names and ages, and where they are at in life." I flipped through my notes. "I can tell you what you have in your estate, what you hope to do with it, what your biggest worries are, and—let's see—quite a bit of other stuff here."

She knew instinctively that I could not possibly help her to make intelligent decisions unless I had enough information. But she had no idea that she had already given me six pages worth of notes. The conversation had been so comfortable that it had seemed like just casual talk. And yet we had accomplished so much already.

I learned long ago in my law practice that people open up so much more when they feel comfortable, and I have made it a priority to create an atmosphere in which all my clients can tell me their needs, their fears, their hopes. It's only when I know these things that I can help to craft a legacy plan that will work for a lifetime and beyond.

—RICK BAILEY

CHAPTER 2
THE FARMER

In this chapter, the following solutions are discussed:

- Limited Liability Company

- Limited Partnership

- Life Insurance

- Dynasty Trust

- Premium Financing

THE SCENARIO

Craig and Linda Lurquin operate a 500-acre farm. He's 58; she's 57. They have five children of whom two think they want to be farmers. Of those two, one is married and is currently working on the farm with his parents. One is still single; he is in school but expects to be coming back and working on the farm. None of the other three children want to be involved at all with the farm operation and have moved away. Two of them are married without children, and one of them is single. So far, there are no grandchildren.

The farm is successful, with a net worth of $15 million. The Lurquins live in an area where the city has been encroaching on the countryside, so part of the farm could potentially be developed. The Lurquins are feeling pressure to decide how to deal with that situation.

THE CHALLENGES

As it stands, the Lurquins have no retirement strategy. Craig and Linda know they need to do something, but they haven't set aside anything for retirement at this point.

Craig and Linda understand that they have a large estate that is growing, and realization has set in that the property could be developed instead of remaining as a farm. They are aware that there is an estate tax, but don't know how that would affect them. From friends and relatives, they have heard that the estate tax could be devastating.

The Lurquins are deeply concerned about the best way to distribute their estate. One of their children is already actively working to grow the farm business, and another likely will be coming aboard to join them, but they want to be fair to all the children. At this point, however, they are not sure what "fair" would look like. On one hand, they would like to see an equal division of their life's work, but they do not know how to balance the fact that two children will be actively participating in the business and three have moved on. Does fair mean equal? Would equal be fair? That is a major concern, and it has been standing in the way of their making decisions.

Craig and Linda are sorely in need of information and guidance. They would like to get these matters resolved, but they aren't certain what decisions need to be made. They know they have let these matters go unattended for a long time. This situation is typical, actually, for a lot of people, and it is especially true for those who have hunkered down and worked hard for decades.

Farmers, typically, are land rich and cash poor. They can have a great year and end up buying additional equipment, feed and seed to offset the current income tax problem. They have some bad years where they struggle to get by. In the Lurquin's case, the value of their land has appreciated dramatically in value over time, meaning the estate's value has blossomed.

Craig and Linda's annual income fluctuates with commodity prices, but they usually have good years. They pride themselves on doing a good job with the income tax planning. They get toward the end of the year and look at what they have made, and they prebuy their feed, their seed, their fertilizer, and their fuel.

It has been said that you can tell the kind of year a farmer has had by taking a look around the farm in December. If the farmer is driving a new truck between Christmas and New Year's, it has been a good year. If he is driving the old truck, it has been a bad year. Farmers tend to control their income tax bill by buying assets, such as equipment and trucks, and depreciating them. However, all that adds to the value of the estate. They do a good job of income tax planning but don't realize that the value of the estate is also appreciating so much.

Due to the way tax laws are set up, buying assets or prepaying expenses is ideal for farmers, who are always needing seed and feed and much more for the upcoming year. They can always buy equipment to offset it. However, that creates a problem when they get to the point of wanting to retire or turn the business over to the children. All those assets have been depreciated for tax purposes. There comes a time when they have to face the question of how they can move their estate to the next generation without burdening the children with a big tax bill that has been pushed from year to year.

Let's say Craig has come to the end of the year and wants to reduce the big tax bill. It has been a good year, and so he buys a new combine for $100,000. The depreciation becomes a write-off against his income. On each of his tax returns over the next few years, Craig deducts a portion of that combine's value until the cost basis has been depreciated down to zero. Then it's time to buy another combine, and he can roll that zero basis into the new combine.

If he sells that combine without replacing it, however, he has to pay ordinary income tax on the amount for which it is sold. By selling the combine, he would "recapture" the depreciation that was taken on previous income tax returns. In other words, if Craig made $500,000 in his business that year, and he sold the combine for $50,000, he would be taxed on $550,000.

Instead of selling the combine, perhaps Craig and Linda decide to gift it to the children. In that case, the children get the basis of whatever assets they receive. Since Craig has depreciated the combine's value to zero, the children will have to pay the tax bill on its $50,000 market value in the year that they sell it—and that will be at the ordinary income tax rate.

If Craig lets the combine flow through the estate, the children get it at fair market value and could sell it the same day and never pay any income tax on it. This type of planning is not a problem for smaller estates with a value below the estate tax exemption. For larger estates, it becomes a question of finding the best time to pass on the property to not only minimize the estate tax but also to take into consideration the income tax for the people receiving the property.

Under current gift tax laws, there are two exemptions that need to be addressed. The first exemption is the annual gift tax exclusion. The annual gift tax exclusion allows you to exempt the first $14,000 per person per year of gifts made. Any amounts above the annual gift tax exclusion would be subject to the gift tax or may be eliminated using the lifetime federal estate or gift tax exemption. This amount is currently $5.43 million per individual or $10.86 million per couple.

Another problem to address is whether the farm is able to support the children who want to stay on to run it and raise their families. Some farm operations can sustain one family but not more. A major concern often is whether the farm can handle the growth.

Another concern for Linda and Craig is who the boss will be when the children return to the farm. Linda and Craig will be transitioning the farm over time and need to decide how and when they will give up control. They have been in control of their affairs for a long time, and they need to make sure the children are capable of taking over the reins. Young people growing up on the farm learn the business step by step, from the time they start feeding the cows to learning to drive a tractor, and possibly, to helping with the books. Farming is probably one of the easiest businesses for transitioning control of the operation.

THE SOLUTIONS

A Limited Liability Company and Limited Partnership

The first solution in a situation such as the one this family faces would be to set up an LLC to control the farm operation. It's a good idea to bring the operation of the business under one roof. Linda and Craig can control the operating LLC and can begin gifting an interest in it to the two sons who want to work the farm. Linda and Craig can start using their annual gift tax exclusion to make these gifts.

In this case Linda and Craig have a $15 million estate that's rapidly appreciating because of the value of the land. It is important to get started in transitioning some of that value and taking advantage of the annual gift tax exclusion—the "use it or lose it" exemption. With Linda and Craig in control of the operating LLC, they can start giving their two sons who want to be involved with the farm a piece of the operation. As long as Linda and Craig maintain control of the LLC, they are in charge of the operation.

But what of the other three children, the ones who do not want to be farmers? This is where we recommend splitting the operation from the assets. To do that, we likely would want to set up a second limited partnership or an LLC that mimics a limited partnership.

Let's look at the limited partnership. Linda and Craig would control it, and they would transfer all of the land inside the limited partnership. Then with the land owned by the limited partnership it could lease the land to the LLC, allowing the LLC to run the farm operation.

What we have created is an operating company and an investment company. The LLC is the company that operates the farm. The limited partnership is the investment company that owns the land and is receiving rental income from the operations. Linda and Craig can now gift an interest in the LLC to the two sons who will be operating the farm. They also would gift an interest in the limited partnership to their other three children.

Meanwhile, even though the children now own part of the estate through the LLC and limited partnership, Linda and Craig still control the land, and they are in charge of the decisions regarding the land and operation. For example, Linda and Craig could own 5 percent of the limited partnership as general partners, with the children owning the other 95 percent as limited partners, but Linda and Craig still would have full control as long as they own the general partnership interest.

This scenario is common in farm planning. With several children in a family, it is never likely that all of them will want to be farmers. An arrangement such as this allows the family business to stay together, with everyone involved as much as they wish and how they wish. It allows the parents to start moving the estate to the next generation while maintaining control of the family business.

Life Insurance

The Lurquins need to assess their ultimate goal. They need to distinguish the farm operation from the real estate investment. Then they can consider those divisions separately in deciding upon a fair way to treat all of their children.

Because Linda and Craig are land rich and cash poor, they need to consider life insurance as a means of eventually equalizing the gifts by giving cash to those children who have left the farm. For one thing, a life insurance payout would make it possible to handle the estate tax bill—and we know a large one is coming. However, the life insurance in this case would play another major role. The two sons who are farming the land would be the beneficiaries of the policy, and they would use the money to buy out their siblings. A buy-sell agreement would be set up in advance to ensure that the buyout would ultimately happen.

After Linda and Craig pass away, the sons who want to be farmers will own the LLC that operates the farm. They will have the life insurance proceeds to buy out their siblings who have the limited partnership but don't want to be farmers. The two sons will end up with both the land and the farm operation, and the other three will be content with the money they get from the deal. The estate has been equalized in the eyes of Linda and Craig.

The buy-sell agreement is critical to this process. Such an agreement determines what will happen in the case of certain triggering events—in this case, the death of Linda and Craig. Other events that a buy-sell agreement might cover include long-term disability, divorce, and bankruptcy. The document affirms what all parties have agreed will happen under the prescribed circumstances.

It's a matter of thinking things through. The siblings already know that some of them want to be farmers and others do not. The land and the tractors and equipment would be of no practical use to those who don't want to farm. However, understandably, they want some cash to compensate them for what they are giving up. Life insurance provides a solution. Whenever there is a land-rich and cash-poor situation, life insurance is an option that can provide the leverage needed to solve the problem.

A FAMILY DIVIDED

I'm fond of farmers. My father was a CPA but also a part-time farmer, and I knew that lifestyle when I was growing up. As a whole, farmers are a down-to-earth bunch. They will stand by one another in times of trouble, but they are also astute and shrewd businesspeople.

If a neighbor's barn catches fire, farmers are quick to help at the first wisp of smoke—but when there's a fire sale, for whatever reason, they are also quick to acquire land and equipment at the best price possible. They watch out for others, and they watch out for themselves.

It's a matter of survival. One year is good, the next horrible, and so much of it is beyond the farmer's control. The best-laid plans can fall victim to the whims of the weather and the world economy. If this way of life is to endure, families must stand united.

Far too often they do not. I have seen families divided in turmoil because one or two of the children want to run the farm, and the others want nothing to do with it. They aren't interested in life on the farm, but they certainly are interested in its monetary value.

I saw one sad scenario in which a farm couple died with no legacy plan in place. They had 400 acres and three sons. One son had stayed with his parents on the land, dreaming of running the farm himself someday, but the other two had long since left to pursue their lives in the big city. Upon their parents' death, however, the two city sons were back on the scene. They went to court and demanded that a judge slice the farm into thirds. They sold off their parcels to a developer. Left with only about 130 acres, their brother lost his livelihood—and his dream.

Had this been handled differently, that young man could be farming to this day and raising his own children on the land while his brothers enjoyed the city life with their fair share. It was all so unnecessary, but without good advance planning, farm families can be divided in such a situation. Brothers and sisters may not speak to one another for the rest of their lives. It's not what their parents envisioned, but unless everyone comes together and finds solutions, it happens all too often.

How, then, can farmers protect their vision for the future and hopes for their families? Farmers, like all of us, need to think hard about their legacy. For some people, that legacy is purely money. They don't see or feel anything beyond the dollar. But by and large, farmers take pride in their way of life and want to preserve it.

Once again, this points to why a business owner must show the leadership that will preserve family unity for generations to come. Without that unity, a way of life will surely vanish. With the right planning, everyone can win, and one day a grandchild may be farming the acres that otherwise might have grown a crop of townhouses.

—RICK BAILEY

Dynasty Trust

A dynasty trust also could come into play as a solution for the Lurquin family. Let's say that instead of gifting an interest to each of the children in the limited partnership, Linda and Craig set up a dynasty trust.

In the dynasty trust, Linda and Craig can stamp their values on the legacy planning and put their vision for the future into clear focus. Once they move the land through the limited partnership into the dynasty trust, that land can stay in the dynasty trust in perpetuity. By protecting the land, they protect the farm operation because the land can never be sold unless it is in the best interests of everyone.

A carefully drafted dynasty trust allows people to design their legacy—how they want future generations to remember them. Through incentives and disincentives, the trust can help to chart the course of their heirs' lives. It's as if you can look over the shoulders of your great-grandchildren and beyond. You can decide what you want to control and influence.

In setting up these arrangements, we help families to design a multigenerational game plan. The dynasty trust can help to accomplish that, along with the LLC, the limited partnership, the life insurance, and numerous other arrows in the quiver. Which of those arrows we pull out will depend upon the client and the client's vision.

Premium Financing

Being rich in land and poor in cash, Linda and Craig might have trouble affording the premiums on an adequate life insurance policy to protect their estate of $15 million. They might have no problem paying the premiums during good years but feel quite pinched during bad years. That's where premium financing is a useful option. It simply means that Craig and Linda go to the bank to finance the purchase of the life insurance.

Think of it like this: Suppose you find the house that you want to buy, and the cost is half a million dollars. You have $1 million in your bank account. Should you pay cash or get a mortgage to purchase the house? Well, if you can invest the money for a return that is higher than the mortgage rate, you probably would want the mortgage—unless you're the kind of person who doesn't like to borrow anything. People and situations are different, so, of course, there is no one answer. It depends.

That's the way it is with premium financed insurance. It depends on the situation. Craig and Linda could get a life insurance policy and pay premiums each year. Or they could go to the bank and get a loan to pay the premiums of the policy. If

Craig and Linda die before the loan is paid off, then part of the death benefit will be used to pay off the loan.

Premium financing is a great tool, especially in such land-rich and cash-poor situations where individuals need the life insurance but may lack the current cash flow to pay the premium. It provides additional leverage to accomplish the vision of passing on the legacy.

HOW IT ALL TURNED OUT

The Lurquins made it a priority that the legacy of the farm would continue. To accomplish that, they proceeded to set up the LLC and the limited partnership. The limited partnership owns the farmland and real estate, with Linda and Craig as the original general partners. The LLC operates the farm and owns all of the equipment and everything associated with the operation. Linda and Craig control the LLC too. The LLC leases the land from the limited partnership.

Now Craig and Linda will start gifting an interest in the LLC annually to the two sons who want to continue farming. They will begin gifting an interest in the limited partnership to the three children who do not want to be farmers. For the time being, they will not be using any of their lifetime estate tax exemption. They want to see how children react to the planning before moving forward.

Ultimately, the couple decided to hold off on setting up a dynasty trust. They wanted to review the situation each year before deciding when it would be appropriate to include a dynasty trust in their legacy planning.

The Lurquins decided to purchase a $10 million second-to-die life insurance policy. Half of that would be used to buy out the three nonfarm siblings from the limited partnership, under the terms of a buy-sell agreement. The remaining $5 million of the payout would be used to allow the other two sons to continue running the farm without a liquidity problem.

CHAPTER 3

THE ORTHODONTIST

In this chapter, the following solutions are discussed:

- Disability Insurance

- Buy-Sell Agreement

- Life Insurance

- Captive Insurance Company

- C Corporation Status

THE SCENARIO

Dr. Earl Strom, a relatively young, self-employed orthodontist, is 48 years old, and his wife Sarah is 47. She handles the books for his practice. They have two children, both in school. They are planning to retire when he turns 60 with enough resources to maintain their lifestyle.

His practice is successful, and he grosses $2 million per year, with a net income of $750,000. He has done some advance planning, and the business has been set up as an S corporation. He has very little debt. He has paid off the equipment for his practice. Their home, which is worth $1.5 million, has a mortgage of $500,000. They have been contributing to the 401(k) at the practice and have a current balance of $225,000.

THE CHALLENGES

As the Stroms look at the amount that they have put away in their 401(k), they know that they are way below their retirement goal. If they are to maintain their lifestyle, they know that they need to do something to increase their savings for retirement.

Dr. Strom is at a point with his practice where he is paying a significant amount of income tax. He has depreciated all of the equipment that he has bought, and now is looking for other ways to reduce the income tax bill.

A major concern for him right now is what would become of his family if he were to die or become disabled, since he is the main provider. How would they move on without him there? How would his wife pay to put their children through college?

And what would become of his practice? His patients depend on his being there for them. If he became disabled without anyone to fill in for him, those patients would soon go elsewhere for treatment and might never return. If he were to die, those patients likewise would soon find another orthodontist. His practice would lose its patient base, and consequently, much of its value. If it could be sold at all, it would go for a fire-sale price. Dr. Strom has worked hard to build up a successful practice, and yet it is unprotected in that regard. The value could vanish.

PRACTICES IN PERIL

The orthodontist was 45 years old, an Eagle Scout who liked to hike, and he seemed to be in great health. But one day, he had a stroke. So often in such situations, the practice is in peril. The clients soon drift off elsewhere while the doctor recuperates.

In this case, he worked with others in his practice who were able to continue follow-up treatments. He was able to go into the office and supervise. Meanwhile, his wife became licensed as a hygienist, and the patients stayed put.

This was a situation in which it all worked out. Still, the consequences of disability are a major issue for a professional practice. The quality and extent of insurance coverage is a critical factor, and it is important to develop relationships and agreements with others in the profession.

—BOB CROSETTO

THE SOLUTIONS

Disability Insurance

Disability insurance, of course, is fundamental to protecting a professional practice, but it is important to take a close look at just what is covered. A lot of orthodontists have group disability coverage that does not cover them in their occupation for a lifetime. The disability policy needs to have the appropriate amount of coverage but also needs to cover the doctors for their specific occupation. In this case, the specific occupation is orthodontics and so the question becomes whether that includes general dentistry. Even though the orthodontist may be able to do general dentistry, is that part of his or her occupation? And so Dr. Strom wants to make sure that the disability coverage is sufficiently inclusive and that he is covered to the amount that he needs and that is specific to his specialty.

Buy-Sell Agreement

Typically, if a practice has two owners, we would recommend a buy-sell agreement that would govern what would happen in the event of death or other specified situations. For example, if one of the doctors were to die, the other one would buy his share of the practice for a set price or a price based on a formula that both parties agree would capture the fair value.

The buy-sell agreement is a contract between the two owners of a business. Anything else that could affect the ownership of the business could be written into the buy-sell agreement—for example, what to do in the event of death, disability, bankruptcy, or divorce.

However, in this situation Dr. Strom does not have a partner. The odds are pretty good, however, that in the same city we could find another orthodontist who is facing the same problem as Dr. Strom. We could propose to that orthodontist that a buy-sell agreement be set up between both practices. If something were to happen to either of them—death, disability, or whatever they specified—then the other would buy out the interest in the practice.

We have thereby solved a problem: both doctors now can move forward, confident in the knowledge that they have a ready, willing, and able buyer for a business that each had worked so hard to build. Such arrangements are not uncommon, and yet many professionals have not solved that problem, and their practice remains at risk as a result. If the doctor were to pass away, an immediate search would have to begin to find a buyer for the practice. In the meantime, much of the value of the practice may dissipate.

Life Insurance

The Strom's two children both hope to attend college, and since both parents have advanced degrees, it would seem likely that their children would pursue advanced degrees as well. That's going to be expensive. Among their options, they could set up a college fund through a 529 plan, which is a tax-deferred savings plan to pay for educational expenses, or the Stroms could take advantage of the ability to grow cash value inside of a life insurance policy, which could work well in this situation. In addition, the life insurance policy can be placed in a trust which would dictate the terms for which the life insurance proceeds could be used.

Life insurance also is going to play a key role in a few other areas. If Dr. Strom were to pass away, the policy would provide the liquidity that the family would need to cover bills if there were a gap in income. We would also look at putting a policy on Sarah, in this case. Even though she does not have the same level of income, she is handling the bookkeeping for the practice and is a significant asset to it. If something were to happen to her, the business would lose her services, and have to hire a replacement. What's more, the family also would likely face an increase in other expenses such as child care. And who would run the children around to their afterschool activities while Dr. Strom was tied up at the office? Would he reduce his hours and thereby reduce his income? There is no doubt that the family would face an increase in such expenses, including ones that they would never have imagined. Having a policy on both husband and wife protects against this problem.

A life-insurance policy can also be designed for supplemental retirement income, in addition to what the couple is already saving in their 401(k). They already know they have a gap in what they will need in retirement. A life insurance policy can build a significant amount of cash value that the couple could access on a tax-free basis for supplemental retirement or whatever they desire. In addition, in the event of a premature death, the retirement plan is self-completing by way of the death benefit.

The money that is saved in a life insurance policy can be accessed at any time, unlike 401(k)s or IRAs in which you have to be at least 59½ years old before you can start withdrawing the money without penalty. And you withdraw money from the policy only if you want to do so, unlike the 401(k)s and IRAs, which require distributions to begin at age 70½.

Even though Dr. Strom is saying he wants to retire early, we have seen that doesn't always happen. Often, the doctor will, instead, gradually cut back. There is an advantage to having money that is available for withdrawal when you want it and only if you want it. That is the case for the money in the life insurance policy—and if it isn't used during life, it will pay out as a death benefit to the beneficiaries, free of income tax.

Captive Insurance Company

An orthodontist faces significant risks in his practice. Those risks could come from a variety of sources: Perhaps there is a breach of client data or, somehow, there is a release of HIPAA information. There might be a problem with a product that the doctor is using. The list of potential risks could be lengthy.

Dr. Strom likely will be self-insuring many of those incidental risks. Alternatively, as we described in chapter 1, he could set up a captive insurance company to cover them. Then he could transfer money as premiums into his captive insurance company. Dr. Strom gets a tax deduction upfront for the cost of the premiums paid.

If none of those risks were to turn into realities, the money would continue to build in his captive insurance company. Over time, that could become a significant amount that he could use to fund his life insurance for supplemental retirement income, or he could use it to buy more equipment or a new building to further build his practice.

Basically, Dr. Strom would be freeing up a lot of money from the expense of ordinary income tax. Let's say he were to pay $200,000 a year for 12 years. Assuming that he faced minimal claims, he would have over $2 million in his captive insurance account. When he did take the money out of the captive, he would be able to do so at the long-term capital gains rate instead of the ordinary income tax rate to which 401(k) withdrawals would be subjected.

Dr. Strom would then reassess whether he wanted to keep contributing to the 401(k). If he could put away enough money either through the life insurance or the captive insurance company or both, would it be worth continuing to fund the 401(k)? Yes, his 401(k) contributions do provide an immediate income tax deduction, but when he pulls that money out at some point, it will be taxed as ordinary income. He will have compounded the problem over time.

With a captive insurance company, you have more control than you do with a 401(k) plan. You have more to say about the taxes that you will pay and when you will have access to the money. By paying premiums of $200,000 into a captive insurance company, Dr. Strom would save $80,000 to $100,000 in income tax, depending on the marginal federal and state income tax rates. As you can see, the opportunity cost of not taking advantage of this would be significant.

C Corporation Status

Dr. Strom was operating his business as an S corporation. However, we recommended that he consider operating as a C corporation. One of the advantages of a C corporation is that he can start deducting some perks, such as medical reimbursement and long-term care, through the corporation on a tax-deductible basis, which he cannot do in an S corporation.

For health-care reimbursements in an S corporation, you have to have medical or dental expenses that are more than 7.5 percent of your gross taxable income in order to include them in your itemized deductions. By contrast, if you have a health reimbursement plan in your C corporation, you can submit those expenses to the corporation, and that becomes a tax-deductible benefit. Depending upon the state where you live, that can mean a savings of 40 to 50 percent in taxes on those expenses.

Once again, it comes down to a matter of control. You gain flexibility. You need to use the right tools, whichever best fit your situation, to most efficiently pull money from your business, and then you need to review those decisions regularly. Tax laws change. Family dynamics change. We can help you make sure that the tools you have chosen still make the most sense for you moving forward.

HOW IT ALL TURNED OUT

Dr. Strom converted the practice from an S corporation to a C corporation. That allowed him to implement a medical reimbursement plan and also to take advantage of tax breaks that C corporations receive.

We found another orthodontist with a similar-size practice and set up a buy-sell agreement between them. In the event of the death or disability of either doctor, the agreement protects them both and also protects the value of their businesses.

We implemented the captive insurance company as recommended. It covers some of the incidental risks of his practice— for example, supply-chain risk, deductions and exclusions on his existing insurance policies, the potential for a client data breach, and regulatory changes that could influence patient reimbursement rates. This arrangement not only covers those risks, but it also provides a significant tax deduction for the practice.

To protect his family, Dr. Strom obtained disability insurance with the maximum coverage allowed. If he were to become disabled, the family would not suffer from the lack of his income. They also obtained two life insurance policies. One of them is designed to build cash value and provide supplemental retirement money that the couple can take out on a tax-free basis. The other policy protects the family in the event of Dr. Strom's death so that Sarah and their children can continue their accustomed lifestyle.

CHAPTER 4
THE HIGH-NET-WORTH COUPLE

In this chapter, the following solutions are discussed:

- Captive Insurance Company
- Limited Liability Company for Real Estate
- Charitable Remainder Trust
- Life Insurance
- Dynasty Trust

THE SCENARIO

As did the couple in the previous chapter, this couple also enjoys a good income from the husband's medical practice. The difference is that these clients are nearing retirement age and have a high net worth: They have made a lot of money through rental and investment properties.

Dr. Daniel Rockford is a 62-year-old surgeon. His wife, Jennifer, is a 60-year-old homemaker who is active in charities. They have three children, all married. So far, they have five grandchildren.

Dr. Rockford is grossing $1.1 million and has $600,000 left after paying all business expenses but before taxes. The couple's monthly expenses are $20,000. His practice is set up as an S corporation. He has been contributing to a 401(k) that currently has a balance of $800,000.

In addition, the Rockfords have $2.2 million of rental property that they hold personally. They also have $2 million worth of investment or development property. Their home is worth $1.2 million, and the mortgage balance is $350,000.

In a few years, when he turns 65, Dr. Rockford wants to start cutting back on the hours that he will be working. By age 70, he wants to be completely retired.

THE CHALLENGES

The Rockfords know when they want to retire, but they are concerned about it despite their high net worth. They want to make sure that they can maintain their lifestyle throughout their retirement years. Jennifer also wants to continue to be active in all of her charitable work. Among their goals is to provide an education for their grandchildren.

They are concerned about liability issues. Dr. Rockford, of course, faces liability risk related to his practice, but as they have built up their portfolio of real estate, they are also starting to see that they face a considerable amount of liability from the rentals.

Daniel and Jennifer also have grown quite tired of the responsibility of arranging for maintenance and repairs of their rentals and dealing with tenants, but they are concerned about what the tax bill would be if they were to sell the rentals. They only paid $500,000 for the properties that now are valued at $2.2 million.

The Rockfords have depreciated the value of those rental properties, not including the land, to zero. Every year, they wrote off a portion of the value on their income tax. Those write-offs greatly reduced their income tax in the years when they took them, but upon the sale of the properties, the government expects that money back. When they sell those properties, the IRS will "recapture" that depreciation, and the gain on the sale will be taxed at the ordinary income rate, not capital gains rates.

Not only does this couple face the double-edged sword of depreciation, but they also are at a point where the estate taxes could be a big issue for them. They are feeling the pressure from all sides. This couple has a high net worth, but even if the value of their estate were under the federal exemption of $5.43 million for each of them, they still must face the state estate tax, which is likely to have a much lower exemption than the federal exemption. In Oregon, the estate tax kicks in with an estate value of $1 million. In the state of Washington, it kicks in at $2 million.

It all adds up to a significant tax bill, but the Rockfords don't know what to do about it. They do not know their options. In such a situation, people sometimes freeze and do nothing. The Rockfords have been putting off the sale of the properties, but continuing to operate the rentals has become a considerable burden. They are facing increased maintenance costs and more investment of their money and time.

They have pushed the tax snowball forward. When they began to push it, the snowball was small. Each year it got bigger. Now all these rental properties are depreciated down to a zero tax basis, and the Rockfords feel trapped. They want to slow down, but they are wondering how they ever will get out of the rental business.

Since Dr. Rockford is a professional with very few write-offs, they already have a high income-tax bill. They're in the highest marginal tax rates. They would like to be able to reduce their tax rate. In the 40 percent bracket, they pay 40 cents to the federal government out of every dollar in income. Including state income tax, the tax could hit closer to 60 cents on the dollar. More than half of their earnings have gone to pay income tax.

THE SOLUTIONS

Captive Insurance Company

One of the first solutions to consider would be setting up a captive insurance company, as explained in earlier chapters, to go along with Dr. Rockford's professional practice.

As a surgeon, Dr. Rockford has a malpractice insurance policy, which has exclusions and deductibles that can be covered by a captive insurance company. He also faces the risk of violations of the HIPAA privacy regulations and the risk of data breach.

Those risks could be significant, and so the captive insurance company that he might set up could call for large premiums. A professional such as Dr. Rockford may be able to justify $200,000 a year in premiums to the captive insurance company. As a rule of thumb in setting up a captive insurance company, 8 to 10 percent of gross earnings can go into premiums. This is just a rule of thumb, and the real amount of premium must be determined by a qualified actuary. Each risk must be identified, quantified, and justified—and in a case such as this, the amount certainly could go well in excess of the rule of thumb.

A nice feature here is that those premiums would be tax deductible for the practice—the S corporation—and would not be treated as taxable income for the captive insurance company. The doctor is setting aside money for potential claims, but if those claims do not arise, then the couple can use that money in their estate and retirement planning.

As for the couple's concerns about liability in the practice and in the rentals, a captive insurance company can provide protection. Basically, a captive can be set up in numerous jurisdictions, either onshore or offshore. There are reasons to take it offshore at times, but typically, a captive will be set up in a state that is more business friendly and has better asset protection laws. There will be protection for assets that are inside the captive insurance company, which is isolated from the professional practice.

It's a great tool with the ability to solve multiple problems. Through coordinated planning, income tax reduction, estate tax reduction, and asset protection can be achieved.

LLCs for the Real Estate

The Rockfords have done what many people do when they get into real estate. They start holding all of the properties personally. The Rockfords have both investment property and rental property, and all of it is held personally. That opens up a lot of potential liability issues.

The first step for the Rockfords would be creating two LLCs, one to hold the $2.2 million in rental property and one to hold the $2 million in investment property. Establishing the two LLCs will provide liability protection. It is important to transfer ownership of the property inside the entity that will protect the couple from liability if someone were to slip and fall or otherwise become injured on the property. We want to make sure that the rental property's liability is encapsulated in that LLC. Also, since we have segregated the investment property from the rentals, we have protected the value of the investment property from a lawsuit against a rental property.

It is important that each LLC be set up so that it is taxed as a partnership. In doing so, the couple's $2.2 million investment within that LLC will have an asset protection wrapper around it. More importantly, the assets can be moved in and out of the LLC without triggering income tax recognition. If the LLC were taxed as a corporation, any time property was moved in or out of that LLC, the tax issue would be triggered.

Some people have an LLC for each parcel of real estate. If they have three rental properties, they have three LLCs. However, it is much easier to set up a series LLC, in which there is a parent LLC that oversees all of the rentals, and then each rental property would be a single member LLC underneath the parent. In this type of plan, the liability is segregated, property by property. A lawsuit would only be able to go after the assets in the one LLC that holds the property involved. But from an accounting and tax reporting standpoint, since single-member LLCs can be "disregarded" for income tax purposes, everything folds up into the parent company. You file one tax return, not 10 or 20 of them.

For someone with a large number of properties, setting up and managing multiple LLCs could become cumbersome. With a smaller number of properties, however, it is a nice way to segregate the liability, asset by asset.

The big question, really, is this: what keeps you up at night? If the liability bothers you, then you are either in the wrong business or you need to set up a business plan that will allow you to protect your assets in a way that allows you to feel comfortable. Let's say you have a dozen rental properties. You could have an LLC for each of them, but then it might be the complexity of the arrangement that keeps you awake. Perhaps, you could get it down to three or four LLCs, combining assets that are relatively similar. Whatever your business design, it should be set up in a way that lets you slumber in peace.

Charitable Remainder Trust

Over time, if the Rockfords really decide to get out of their real estate holdings, one of the best tools for doing that is a charitable remainder trust. The Rockfords could transfer their $2.2 million of rental properties into it, designate a beneficiary, and the trust would sell the property. Since the trust is a charitable entity, the sale would not trigger any income taxes. If the Rockfords were to sell that property outside of the charitable trust, they would lose about half of its value, or at least $1 million, to taxation.

The Rockfords could reinvest the proceeds from the sale of the real estate into other assets that wouldn't require them to fix toilets anymore for surly tenants. Through the trust, they could invest the proceeds in stocks, bonds, other types of commercial real estate, and so on. The charitable remainder trust would begin paying the couple an annuity stream at the percentage they choose at the time the trust was established. The annuity stream could be paid over a set number of years or over their joint lifetimes.

Let's say, for example, the percentage is 5 percent. Each year, the trust would pay them 5 percent of the value within the trust. On $2 million, that would bring them $100,000 a year. Had they sold the property outside the trust and thereby netted only $1 million after taxes, their income stream would be only $50,000 a year for that same 5 percent return. This tax strategy has doubled their retirement income. They will be living far better on money that they otherwise would, essentially, have been paying Uncle Sam.

At the end of the trust term, whatever is left in the trust would be distributed to the designated charity or charities—in their case, the ones to which Jennifer had long devoted her time. In effect, then, the couple could get an annuity for the rest of their lives and still benefit their chosen charities.

Some assets, however, would not go into a charitable remainder trust. For example, if you have a historic property that has been in the family for 100 years, you likely would want to keep that property in the family and not sell it. You would therefore not want it to go into a charitable remainder trust. You would want that property to pass through the estate. In the case of the Rockfords, however, their rental properties are more of a commodity. They want to exchange their real estate for other investable assets that do not require so much management on their part.

By placing the property in the charitable remainder trust, they can reduce their tax liability and enhance their assets for retirement. Again, we choose the right tool for the right goal. We find out what our clients hope to accomplish, and then we find the specific planning strategy that will get them there.

"NOW THAT I THINK ABOUT IT ..."

On a number of occasions, I have suggested to people that they consider charitable planning. "Well, we are not really charitably inclined," they sometimes say.

"If you would like, I will choose the charity for you, because in your situation it makes perfect sense, financially, for you to do this." I explain to them that their heirs will not be deprived and that, in fact, their children can come out way ahead through a charitable giving strategy.

Once I present it in that light, the attitude often changes: "Well, yes, now that I think about it, we do have charities that we would like to support." The turning point is when they realize that it's not "A or B" but rather, it is "A and B." Once they understand that they can give to others without depriving themselves and their heirs, they can certainly think of causes to which they would like to contribute. They may not, at first, have felt inclined toward charity, but they are certainly inclined toward common sense.

Charitable giving can be to a university endowment fund, to its athletic program, or to any 501(c)(3) organization. The money can go into a general fund, or it can go into something specific, such as scholarships. The only restriction is that the charity has to agree to accept the gift, which, of course, most charities are more than happy to do.

You can also set up charitable giving so that the money goes into your own private family foundation, which will manage the money and over time, distribute it to whichever charities the foundation decides to support. If you have a large estate, you may not wish for all of the money to go as one big gift to, say, the Red Cross or the Salvation Army. Instead, the family foundation can choose the charities annually.

At the time you set up the gift, you can decide, "Do I want this to be a revocable beneficiary or an irrevocable designation?" Most people want to have the flexibility of a revocable designation. For example, at one point they might designate a gift for their favorite college—but then their children go to a different college, and now they want to funnel some of the money over there. Or, perhaps, the mission of the charity changes to the point where the giver no longer feels supportive. Maybe the mission stays the same but the giver no longer subscribes to the same beliefs or has developed new interests and a new charitable passion.

Charities change, and people change, and most charities have no problem with a revocable designation that would allow such flexibility.

The charitable remainder trust itself is irrevocable once it has been set up. However, what the donor can retain is the ability to change the beneficiary. You have committed to contribute "X" amount of dollars to charity, but you still want to pick and choose who gets the money. With a charitable remainder trust, the beneficiary can be a private foundation that regularly reviews and selects the causes and institutions that it deems worthy. The giving can become a family decision.

—RICK BAILEY

Life Insurance

Upon seeing how a charitable remainder trust works, some people say that the only charity they really want to benefit is their family. They protest that they do not want to cut their children out of the deal. With proper planning, that need not be the case at all.

With the income stream they get from the charitable remainder trust, the Rockfords could invest in a life insurance policy. The proceeds of that policy would replace the bequest that is going to charity instead of to the children.

Having moved $2.2 million of property into the charitable remainder trust, the Rockfords now can get a life insurance policy for, perhaps, several million dollars, naming their children as beneficiaries. To pay for the policy, they would use part of the charitable tax deduction savings from the gift to the charitable trust.

In this way, Dr. and Mrs. Rockford could divest themselves of their real estate holdings without triggering a big tax burden. They would also be benefiting charities about which they have long felt passionate. In doing so, in no way have they shortchanged their family. The children would get their inheritance, free of both income and estate tax, via the life insurance policy. In fact, the policy could provide them a far greater gain than they would have received through a direct inheritance.

Life insurance in combination with a charitable remainder trust is a great strategy for the right kind of client. The strategy exemplifies the powerful and flexible nature of life insurance.

The Rockfords' goals include paying for a college education for each of their grandchildren. We have discussed previously the power of a life insurance policy to efficiently provide money for that purpose. In setting up such a strategy, the Rockfords will have flexibility regarding whose name is on the policy as the owner, insured, or beneficiary. The insurance could be on the grandchildren, or it could be on Jennifer and Daniel—whatever best fits into the planning. The couple maintains control. They need not turn that control over to anyone else.

They also could set up a survivorship life insurance policy and overfund it, building up a lot of cash value. A survivorship policy can insure the lives of both parents, and the death benefit is paid out at the time the second parent dies. During retirement, it would add to the potential cash available to the Rockfords. They could either turn it on as an income stream, or they could use it as their "what if?" bucket of money for whatever needs or desires arise. Should they decide to take a world tour, the money in the policy would be there for them on a tax-free basis.

Of course the cost of the life insurance policy will depend on the insured's age and health. The insurance underwriting should be finalized prior to executing the plan. We want to make sure in advance that every piece fits.

In this case, both Daniel and Jennifer are in good health. Even if one of them were not in good health, the policy could be written on the other. The insurance can be for either, both, or combined in a second-to-die policy. Let's say a wife is in good health but her husband is uninsurable. Combining them on one policy will reduce the costs to a level that a couple can afford.

Life insurance is less expensive for younger people, but it still makes sense to consider it when you are in your 60s, 70s, or even 80s. In the last several years, insurance companies have had to reprice their policies because of the change in mortality tables. People are living longer. The cost of insurance has dropped. Life insurance continues to be a valuable tool for exchanging dollars that would otherwise be subject to income and estate taxes to tax-free.

Life insurance, as a financial instrument, is probably the least understood instrument out there. It can provide an incredible amount of leverage for legacy planning.

The Dynasty Trust

The Rockfords can now put in place a dynasty trust into which they can move property and draft incentive language that provides for the education of their grandchildren as well as potential health-care needs. Through the dynasty trust, the Rockfords can encourage and discourage certain behaviors to make sure that "their" money is used over time in a way that conforms to their beliefs. That can continue for multiple generations, as long as money remains in the trust.

HOW IT ALL TURNED OUT

The first step for this high-net-worth couple was to set up a captive insurance company for Dr. Rockford's operating business. As we have seen, that arrangement will cover outstanding risks, such as deductibles and exclusions on existing insurance policies and also protect the business from potential claims if client information was stolen.

Daniel and Jennifer also set up limited liability companies to hold their portfolio of real estate. Doing so in the proper way provides both asset protection and management control for the properties. Because the Rockfords told us that they wanted to start eliminating some of their real estate in three years, they plan to set up a charitable remainder trust at that point. The charitable remainder trust will provide them with an annuity stream during their retirement years, after which the money will go to their favorite charities.

The Rockfords established a dynasty trust with provisions benefiting their children and grandchildren. Some of their real estate they will transfer right away to the dynasty trust. Then they will be able to purchase a $5 million life insurance policy to protect the estate. After they set up the charitable remainder trust, they will purchase another life insurance policy. The proceeds of the policy will replace that wealth given to charity inside the dynasty trust.

CHAPTER 5

THE FAMILY BUSINESS OWNER

In this chapter, the following solutions are discussed:

- Setting Up a Corporation
- Setting Up Limited Liability Companies
- The Family Office
- Captive Insurance Company
- Key-Man Insurance Policies
- Irrevocable Trust or Dynasty Trust

THE SCENARIO

This is a family business that happens to be a manufacturing company, but there are thousands of such closely held businesses of many descriptions. Self-employed people face many pressures, but there are many creative strategies—many arrows in the quiver—to help them.

Rick Hendrickson is 55, and his wife, Becky, is 54. They have a net worth of $20 million, and the majority of their net worth is due to the appreciation of the land and the building for the business.

They have four children. Two of them are in college. One has graduated from college but is not in the business. The fourth is a child with special needs. As of yet, they have no grandchildren.

The manufacturing company owns the building and the land, and it also owns a fleet of vehicles. The company nets $1.5 million per year, and the salary for Rick is $600,000.

Rick has been contributing to his company 401(k) plan. The account has been growing, but it will not be enough to maintain their lifestyle during retirement.

THE CHALLENGES

The Hendricksons are deeply concerned about what will become of their child with special needs. They have done a great job taking care of him, and they know that programs are available to benefit him. The Hendricksons want to design their legacy plan with an emphasis on providing the best quality of life possible for their child, but at the same time, they want to be fair to all of their children and try to equalize the estate.

How will they accomplish that? In many such situations, the distribution simply is not equal. Perhaps their special needs child will need 40 percent of the entire estate value to take care of him for the rest of his life. All the siblings might be perfectly happy if their sibling with special needs gets that much of the estate, because they will be successful business owners in their own right. Nonetheless, the goal will be to enhance the benefits for everyone. The distribution might not be equal, but it should be equitable and fair in the eyes of Rick and Becky.

A big question here is who will physically provide the care for their special needs child. Will he be going into an institution? Is home care an option? Might one of the siblings become the caretaker?

As we are seeing so often throughout this book, the issue, in essence, is control. That is a fundamental consideration when dealing with the problems of any large estate, and it is particularly true for a closely held business. The strategy must be structured to maintain as much control as possible.

In this case, not only does the couple need a strategy to maintain control of the manufacturing business, but they also need a strategy that will ensure the family maintains control of the well-being of their special needs child. That is a concern that will affect every member of the family, and the goal is to find the tools to deal with this situation in the most efficient and caring way. It is an emotional issue as well as a financial one. This is a matter of love. Rick and Becky want to ensure that the caretaker provides the kind of attention and compassion that they would give their child if they were still on earth.

As for the issue of control in regard to the manufacturing company, Rick has long held the reins, controlling the processes and the investment. When does he give it up and to what extent? As the company grows, what are the implications for estate tax? If Rick were to die or for some reason become unable to lead the company, how would it survive? Who would pay the mortgage, the business loans? Who would provide for the family?

The Hendricksons need to have a transition plan in place. The business generates all the money for the estate. It is the source of the family's livelihood. If the business suffers, the estate suffers. If the business is protected, the family's income likely will remain in place. That will require a smooth and proper transition.

THE SOLUTIONS

Setting Up a Corporation

Rick has done a great job in building up the family business, and he has run it as a sole proprietorship. The first thing is to examine the potential benefits of changing the operation from a sole proprietorship to a corporation.

One good reason for making this change would be to put a box around the liabilities that the business generates. It is important to start providing some asset protection for the rest of the estate.

What sort of corporation entity should Rick establish? We most certainly would want to sit down with his accountants and take a close look at whether an S corporation or a C corporation would be the best option. One is not necessarily better than the other. Each solves certain needs at certain levels.

Setting Up LLCs

Rick should establish two LLCs. One LLC would hold the land and the building. The other LLC would hold the vehicles. Then the operating company would rent the real estate and vehicles from the LLCs.

The rental agreement for the real estate would be structured as a triple-net lease, which would give all of the burden of operating the building to the corporation. If, for some reason, the corporation were to be sued, the land and the building would be a protected asset in the LLC.

Why put the vehicles in a separate LLC all by themselves? The reason is twofold. Every day, those vehicles are on the road, with drivers heading out in all directions. If someone were to get into an accident, a lawsuit could make a major claim on the estate if the titles were held by Rick and Becky. That is why we want to isolate those vehicles from the other assets. On the other hand, in the event that the corporation would face a lawsuit, those vehicles would be a protected asset in their own LLC.

The structure would give Rick and Becky the ability, at retirement, to sell the business while also keeping the land and the building and the vehicles for rental income. They could sell the whole package, but this arrangement would give them further flexibility to decide what would be best for their family. The rental income stream could be quite useful.

Also, now that the LLCs are set up, Rick and Becky can start gifting part of them to the children using the annual gift tax exclusions or the lifetime exemptions.

The Family Office

As the children start to become part owners of the LLCs, Rick and Becky will have the opportunity to set up a family office. They will be able to begin talking to their children as fellow business owners.

As is the case in many family businesses, the children were not even on the horizon back when Rick and Becky launched the company. The children didn't see the struggles of those early days. They were not witness to how their parents built the business and did their best to keep up the cash flow. They were unaware of all those calls from the bank.

Now, as the children become part of the business, the family office structure will help to ensure that they do become aware. Rick and Becky can communicate how they make decisions and why. They can explain why the family is in this particular type of enterprise. They can explain why they are investing in certain types of assets. In short, they can begin to train the next generation on how to be good businesspeople.

The Captive Insurance Company

For Rick and Becky, we will also revisit the solution of the captive insurance company. Since this is a manufacturing business, it faces a variety of operational risks as well as potential problems with its products and consumer claims.

The business no doubt deals with a large commercial insurance company for typical major risks, but for other risks that cannot be insured that way, it is allowed to set up its own captive insurance company, administered and operated in much the same way as the big ones.

Captive insurance companies are meant to deal with the kind of claims that have a low probability of occurring, not the potentially devastating claims that third-party insurance companies would cover. Those big insurers are also a readily available source for coverage such as workers compensation or auto insurance, which is relatively inexpensive insurance for what it provides.

Other insurances are best suited for a captive. A business could face liability, for example, from a data breach of its clients' confidential information, even if it is using the most up-to-date software and has rules and procedures in place. The money that builds up within a captive insurance company would provide the reserves to take care of such a claim.

Warranty claims are another example of a risk that can be handled through the captive. How often have you been asked whether you want an extended warranty on some product—a computer, a cell phone, a car? That extended warranty program, more than likely, is being run through a warranty captive insurance company.

Most large corporations have captive insurance companies, and they have become available to smaller businesses as well.

Businesses face liabilities that they cannot economically insure elsewhere, and this gives them an opportunity to transfer that risk to an insurance company that they set up themselves. In the event that there are no claims, then they can pocket the profit.

Key-Man Insurance Policies

Our primary objective for Rick and Becky is to protect the company and to protect their revenue streams. Toward that end, they need to make sure that the company could continue regardless of any number of contingencies. Rick and Becky have identified two crucial employees to the business. The business should have a key-man insurance policy on each of them.

The reason is quite simple: If either of those key people were to pass away, there would be a substantial hole in the business. It would need to be filled immediately. The key-man insurance policy would provide the liquidity to immediately hire a replacement. The policy would provide the necessary cash, free of income tax. The security of that coverage would play a key role in maintaining the company's integrity.

Irrevocable Trust or Dynasty Trust

The couple still needs a solution for dealing with their child who has special needs. A good choice to put in place here would be an irrevocable trust, or preferably, a dynasty trust.

Inside an irrevocable trust, provisions called special-needs language can be added. That special-needs language could tell the trustee, in effect, "Look at the needs of this child. To the extent possible, let's take advantage of governmental programs that are available to benefit children such as ours. However, if those benefits do not cover all of our child's needs, then you are authorized to use all available assets within this trust to do whatever it takes to care for him."

If this is set up as a dynasty trust, that directive could continue for multiple generations, as long as assets are available. It could cover the care not only of this particular child but also of children with special needs in future generations.

Rick and Becky's goals will determine how this is set up. How do they want the money to be used? The special needs language gives the trustee the discretion to treat the money in the same way that Rick and Becky would have wanted it to be used if they were still alive. The irrevocable trust can provide that protection—and with a dynasty trust, that protection can continue, generation to generation, as long as the money lasts.

A dynasty trust also could own the captive insurance company. That way, the profits that are generated through the captive insurance company would flow right into the dynasty trust. There would be no gift tax issues, and there would be no estate tax issues.

Because Rick and Becky have such a large net worth, they would otherwise face a substantial gift tax. This is a business transaction by which dollars can be moved through the captive insurance company into the dynasty trust without any gift tax. Why? Because the intent is not to make a gift. When the corporation pays the premium to the captive insurance company, the intent is to acquire insurance coverage. When there are no claims, the resulting profit is distributed to the owner of the captive insurance company—which is the dynasty trust.

With the trusts and the other solutions, coordination is again the key. Once we know the goals, then we can bring together a variety of tools and identify ways for them to work together to meet those goals. People can maintain control as long as they want or as long as they are alive and able. We give them their options, and they can pick and choose what will work best. We are the catalyst for action to complete their legacy planning.

HOW IT ALL TURNED OUT

Rick and Becky set up an S corporation to operate the business instead of a sole proprietorship. This provides asset protection for the company, and it provides the corporate structure in case Rick and Becky want to sell the business later.

Rick and Becky also established two limited liability companies, one to hold the land and buildings and the other to hold the vehicles. Leases between the corporation and LLCs were structured so that the corporation rents the property and retains the liability.

Rick and Becky set up an annual gifting program to transfer shares of the LLC to their children. That sets the scene for creating a family office through which Becky and Rick can begin to train the children to take care of the assets that they will be inheriting.

In addition, the corporation now has a captive insurance company. This provides a greater degree of risk coverage, along with the opportunity for tax deductions for the business.

Rick and Becky identified four key employees who are essential to the business so that the corporation could buy life insurance and disability policies on them. If any of them were to pass away or become disabled, the business would have the cash flow to immediately acquire additional help without a disruption in profitability.

The couple now has a dynasty trust. Becky and Rick have identified the values that they want to pass on to future generations, and the trust includes incentive language to help make it so. For their child with special needs, they included a special provision that lets the trustee allocate whatever is needed to take care of him the way Becky and Rick would have done if they were alive.

Finally, to handle the estate taxes that they anticipate when both have died, they have purchased a $10 million life-insurance policy inside the dynasty trust. The trustee will be able to use the insurance proceeds to take care of the estate taxes that will be due upon their death, and the policy also will provide benefits to future generations through the dynasty trust.

CHAPTER 6

THE MARKETING ORGANIZATION

In this chapter, the following solutions are discussed:

- Setting Up a Limited Liability Company
- Setting Up a Family Office
- Captive Insurance Company
- Life Insurance

THE SCENARIO

Ben Martin is 52, and his wife, Kathy, is 48. Together, they operate a network marketing business. Both are active in the business, but Kathy is the one who drives it. They have one son and two daughters, all of whom are out of school, and one of them is working with them in the business. Two of their children are married, and they have one grandchild.

The business is structured as a sole proprietorship. The gross revenue is $800,000 a year. The business expenses are $5,000 a month or $60,000 a year. The couple's living expenses are $20,000 a month. Their home is worth $1 million, with a mortgage of $350,000. They also have a vacation home that is worth $600,000, with a mortgage of $420,000.

Many people had another business or profession before they got involved in network marketing. We know one gentleman who was a butcher until he injured his back. He is now 85 years old and making $2 million to $3 million a year in network marketing.

In this case, Ben had worked full time as a laborer, and Kathy started this business on the side to supplement their income. It wasn't long before her income exceeded his, and he retired. Today, their income is about 20 times what he had been earning as a laborer.

THE CHALLENGES

Ben's salary and retirement had been orchestrated. The company told him how much he would be paid and how long he would be able to work there. Not so with this new endeavor. The income and the retirement are not so defined.

A lot of people misunderstand network marketing and think that you work hard for five years and then just head for the beach. This couple has been working long and hard, and they want to get to the point where they can reduce those hours, although not retire in the traditional sense. In doing so, they want to maintain the lifestyle to which they have become accustomed.

They have limited financial and business experience, despite the success of their endeavor. They do understand that something should be done about their current income tax bill. And it seems as if every time Ben puts his toe in the water, trying to invest in something, they lose. Where Ben and Kathy consistently make money is in their business and in their real estate.

Almost everyone in network marketing has, at some point, been with a company that was mismanaged, that cut their income, or that went bankrupt. That happened to Ben and Kathy, once, with a prior company. Ben and Kathy are somewhat worried about whether something could happen at the parent company that would affect their future. They would like to have a contingency plan.

Ben and Kathy want to be able to transfer the business to their children one day. Since one of their children is already in the business and understands it, it is quite likely that this could continue as a family enterprise for generations.

THE SOLUTIONS

Setting Up an LLC

The first tool to employ for Ben and Kathy would be a limited liability company. They have a large income. They have substantial assets growing. As they start to accumulate other assets, they could manage all of those investments—real estate, stocks and bonds, or whatever—inside the structure of an LLC that is designed for that purpose.

The LLC provides the opportunity for the family office, as we explain in the next section, and it also will provide asset protection. In case there is a lawsuit against the network marketing company, Ben and Kathy now have set aside those assets inside the LLC. And so the LLC provides a management structure, and it provides asset protection.

One son and one daughter are currently not involved in the network marketing business. The son operates a construction business, and the daughter is a homemaker and has Ben and Kathy's only grandchild. Through the LLC, Ben and Kathy now have the potential to partner with their son directly on construction projects, or they can operate as the bank for his projects and start lending him money. This gives them added flexibility in deciding how the relationship will be built. A captive insurance company, once it is mature, also could serve as the bank for some of those investments.

Setting Up a Family Office

A first major step for this company would be to set up their operation as a family office. Because a lot of people come to the field of network marketing from other pursuits, they often lack a firm grasp of business fundamentals. By setting up a family office, Ben and Kathy will be truly operating as a business. This will be a good opportunity to further develop their children's knowledge of the business. It will provide a setting in which everyone can begin to understand the decisions that need to be made and whether to bring in an attorney, a CPA, a banker, a financial planner, or whomever they need for counsel and assistance.

Captive Insurance Company

Since this is a business that's making a great income with very few expenses, a captive insurance company could be quite beneficial. Even though this couple is involved in marketing, there are risks involved in this business. What about the supply chain? What would happen to their business if the parent company were to start having problems with delivering product? What happens if something harms the parent company's reputation? What if there is a change in government regulations related to the products that they are marketing?

The Martins certainly would be able to identify a variety of risks that would qualify for coverage in their own captive insurance company. As has been the case for so many of the people whom we have spotlighted in these chapters, Ben and Kathy could enjoy the benefits of transferring money as premiums out of their operating company and into the captive insurance company on a tax-deductible basis.

If any of those risks were to occur, they would have reserves set aside to cover them. If they did not occur, the pool of money would, nevertheless, be there so that they could continue their business, whether with the same parent company or a different one. The captive insurance company, in effect, would serve as a bucket of safe money so that the family could be confident about maintaining its standard of living.

Ben and Kathy have been considering setting up a 401(k) or an IRA. Both can be great tools. But there is a potential problem with the fundamental presumption on which they are based, and that is that people make less money in retirement than during their working years. You get an immediate tax deduction for the amount that you contribute to these retirement plans. Through the years, the investments within the plan will grow, and you will continue to get deductions for contributions and will not have to pay tax until you begin to withdraw the money for retirement income. The presumption is that, during retirement, you are in a lower tax bracket than during your earning years.

However, that certainly isn't always the case. Network marketers, for example, never seem to hit that magical retirement age. They don't just turn 65 and walk out the door. If they have been successful, they want it to continue. Their business ends up growing, not slowing, during their retirement years. Their income soars, and soon they reach the age of 70½, when the government requires them to take increasingly large annual distributions from that 401(k) or IRA. All of that money is taxable as ordinary income, and they are now at the highest of brackets. The deferral has resulted in a higher tax, not a lower one.

Now, consider what happens when you pay premiums to your own captive insurance company to cover the potential for risks. When you pay the premium, you get a deduction from your ordinary income tax. The money then moves out of the operating company and into the captive. When you withdraw it from there, the tax is at the capital gains rate, not the higher ordinary income tax rate. And you control the timing of that withdrawal and taxation.

In this type of a situation, when you compare a 401(k) or IRA to the benefits of a captive insurance company, the latter seems to make more sense. The captives have a double advantage of being more flexible as well as offering a tax savings that you don't have with those retirement plans. With the 401(k)s and IRAs, you are penalized for early withdrawal before age 59½. There is no such penalty for taking a withdrawal from a captive insurance company. And if you do not need the money, you are not forced to withdraw it when you reach 70½.

Life Insurance

In this situation, life insurance would serve two purposes. The Martins have developed a significant net worth, so life insurance is an important supplement in the event that one or both of the spouses passes away prematurely.

In addition, they could start building up cash value inside a life insurance policy to help provide supplemental income for retirement. Ben and Kathy have expressed some concerns about the stability of the parent company of their business, and so the life insurance cash value amounts to a "what if" bucket of money. "What if" something goes wrong? "What if" they decide to take a trip around the world? This provides a nice safety net in case of a premature death, but it also can provide the cash flow for many other needs and desires.

The life insurance policy gives them the ability to grow money, tax deferred, that they can access at any time income tax-free. It's not like a qualified retirement plan in which they cannot touch the money until age 59½ without a penalty and are required to begin taking it out at 70½.

Many people who get into network marketing and become successful think the goose that lays that golden egg is never going to die. They continue to spend what they are making. And then, if something goes wrong and they do not have sufficient money set aside, either in a captive insurance company, life insurance policy, or investments, they can be in trouble.

If all goes well, and they continue to make money and never need to take a withdrawal from their life insurance, obviously there would be a benefit that would go to their heirs. They can do that earlier, however, whenever they wish to give up control of it. The money can go into a trust or be transferred to the heirs.

In addition, life insurance in many states is asset protected. You have control of that asset, but you still have liability protection for it. And when you decide that it is time to move it on to the next generation, you can readily do so.

HOW IT ALL TURNED OUT

The Martins set up a limited liability company and moved the marketing company inside of the LLC. The LLC was structured in such a way that it could pass from one generation to the next and protect the legacy for the children and grandchildren.

With the LLC in place, Ben and Kathy were able to gift a small percentage of the LLC to each of their children using their annual gift tax exclusion. The LLC allowed them to set up a family office, so they could start training their children on how to build the organization on their own.

Ben and Kathy also set up a captive insurance company, which gave the company a deduction for insurance premiums of $150,000 per year. A major risk that they face—and that the captive will handle—is supply chain risk. Any hiccup in their supply chain, in which product moves to customers, could significantly drain their income. And so the captive insurance company serves the dual purpose of protection and tax management.

Outside the company, Ben and Kathy purchased a life insurance policy for $2 million of death benefit protection. It was designed to grow the cash value inside the policy for supplemental retirement income and to be a legacy to pass on to the children. If the marketing organization continues to grow, Ben and Kathy will not be needing that money—but the policy takes care of the "what if's,"—not only the question of "what if we die?" but also "what if we keep on living and need the additional money?"

THE HIGH-INCOME EMPLOYEE

Employees, no matter how high their income level, have very little control over tax issues—and they are subject to an enormous amount of tax because their salary is counted as ordinary income.

They have little in the way of flexibility, and yet employers may be willing to find ways to help them, particularly when they are dealing with key personnel who would be difficult to replace.

One planning vehicle would be an executive bonus arrangement. The employer could set up a life insurance policy for the employee. To fund it, the employer would either put additional compensation into the premium for the policy or arrange a salary reduction agreement with the employee.

The employee would be the owner of the policy, and the money inside that policy now would be growing tax deferred. The employee could access it tax-free through either loans or withdrawals. To cover the taxes related to the amount of premium that the employer pays, the employee would either take a loan from the policy or, perhaps, receive bonus money to cover those taxes.

It is a nice benefit for the employee, but it is subject to what the employer is willing to do. If you are a highly paid key employee, you are no doubt very valuable to the organization. You might approach your employer and suggest that these are some benefits to consider—a stock ownership plan, a deferred compensation plan, or an executive bonus plan. Your employer might be quite receptive to learning more about the possibilities.

—RICK BAILEY

CONCLUSION

THE DREAMING AND THE DOING

In this book you have met a variety of people striving for the good life and dreaming of a prosperous future, for themselves and for generations to come. These are people who were determined to find ways to make the most of their resources so that they might do their best for their family and for the causes they care about.

Certainly all of us want our loved ones to benefit from our years of hard work, and we would like to leave them a legacy, but we also want to know that they will use it prudently. We don't want to leave a gift that they will squander or that will squelch their ambitions. We would like them to use it to advance the dreams we had for them and for humanity.

In short, we want to make sure that the money does good, not harm. Sure, we might accomplish that by leaving it all to charity, particularly if we observe that our children are not in want. But what about our children's children and the generations hence? Would we not want the money to be available for a special need should it arise one day? Suppose a great-grandson needs an expensive but lifesaving operation. Would you want money set aside for that contingency? Many, many years from now, someone in your family may be in dire need and could benefit greatly from the fruits of your life's work. You can make it happen if you take action now.

You can be assured that you will die one day. The fountain of youth is as elusive as ever. And yet you can have a great deal to say about what becomes of all those resources you worked a lifetime to gather. You need not leave it to the whims of the government, and you need not leave it unprotected to be misused by heirs who do not share your vision.

You have options. Most people have a good heart. They want to help. They just don't know how. For many people, the only thing holding them back is that they don't know where to start. Ask yourself this: If you could do something to benefit both your family and the causes and institutions that you cherish, why wouldn't you?

Many people know full well that they have some issues that they need to resolve. Rest assured, there are those to whom you can turn for expert guidance. Some people worry about how much that guidance might cost, but the cost of inaction will certainly be far greater. Some feel intimidated. Some are such perfectionists that they want everything to be perfect before they start—and so they procrastinate.

They may be wary of giving up even an iota of control. And so they put it off, and they put it off, and one day it's too late. The influence that they could have had for generations to come is lost forever.

For those who do envision a legacy, what they need is a means of making it all come together. The first step is to determine what that legacy would look like, if nothing were standing in the way. How would they wish to influence the lives of their children and grandchildren and great-grandchildren? How would they wish to leave their mark on the community? Once they are clear about that, then we can orchestrate the mechanism to get there.

Some people surf the web and actually believe that they can set themselves up adequately by filling out some do-it-yourself documents. The tools that we have described in this book are incredible instruments—if they are structured correctly. If they are structured incorrectly, they can be worse than useless. It's like buying an ill-fitting shoe off the shelf. You soon will be limping. You need a shoe designed from the best materials, custom fitted, and crafted with pride.

You have a lot of money at stake and there are so many variables that could play into your particular situation. That is why most people have an assortment of advisors. We are not here to step on anyone's toes. We are here to give you the view from 30,000 feet, a perspective that virtually always seems to be missing when we begin to work with people just like you.

We are here to coordinate all of those experts that you already have in place—your CPA, your attorney, your investment advisor, your real estate agent, and so on—not to replace them. In our experience, it is rarely the case that any of them are in touch with the others. The right hand doesn't know what the left hand is doing. It takes a collaborating team, with a conductor, to accomplish the important task of planning your legacy.

Think of us as the catalyst. We make sure that things happen once everything is in place. We cut through the confusion and the excuses. We make sure people move their project to completion, until it is done to their satisfaction. We motivate. You might call us your accountability coach.

Without coordination and follow-through, you might have a trust here and an LLC there and a life insurance policy somewhere else, and all to no avail. Our aim is to help you save money that you may unknowingly be wasting. And since there are many places where that can happen, we are here to make sure that the right tools are employed at the right time with the help of the right people.

You can't just walk in and ask us to hand you a legacy plan. It's not as if we can blow the dust off one that is lying around on a shelf. We could give you Frank's legacy plan, and if you happen to look just like Frank, then, perhaps, it would work for you.

Or you could settle for the default legacy plan that the government will gladly provide for you, but you probably wouldn't want that one either, unless you have money to burn. You could just let the government collect as much as possible from you in tax revenue and distribute it, as it sees fit, to its own "charities." However, you might not be all that enamored of the politicians' predilections.

Instead, we help you reclaim the control and the choice. We develop your legacy plan by working backward from your goals. We need to know how, in a perfect world, you would want your life's work to be passed on to your heirs. And then we get down to the tax rules and legal structures to accomplish those ends.

In no way is this tax evasion. We are talking about perfectly legitimate tax breaks that the government has put in place to encourage free enterprise and personal initiative. In the words of the renowned federal judge and judicial philosopher Learned Hand, "There is nothing sinister in so arranging one's affairs as to keep taxes as low as possible."

It's time to stop holding a match to your money. It's time to stop burning up your legacy. As you have seen repeatedly in these pages, you can do much to stop the wanton waste and to preserve your hard work for posterity, by saving a fortune in taxes or by whatever means. Those savings could double, and double, and double again, for generations. A million dollars tucked away now in a dynasty trust, free of taxes, is likely to become $2 million in a decade and to eclipse a billion dollars within a century. Do the math. That's a legacy worth the dreaming and the doing.

CONTACT US

We hope this book will encourage you to review your family and business legacy plan with confidence. The overall theme of the book is planning flexibility and control.

www.OrchestrateYourLegacy.com

800-283-0647

We are available to talk over your concerns and answer any questions.

APPENDIX

ESTATE PLANNING FUNDAMENTALS

The place to start any legacy plan is with basic estate planning documents. These documents act as an umbrella over all of the other planning. This would include a will or revocable trust. These documents dictate who is going to inherit the main part of the estate and take into account the use of the federal estate tax exemption.

The choice of whether to use a will or a revocable trust as the backbone of the estate plan will usually depend on the state where you live. If property passes to the heirs through the will, this process involves probate. Many states have streamlined probate processes for efficiency. However, some states have onerous probate laws or make the process public, which may cause people to consider using a revocable living trust to pass property to their heirs.

In addition to the will or revocable trust that will provide the backbone of the estate plan, each individual should also have a power of attorney to appoint the person or persons who will make decisions regarding property and healthcare decisions in case of mental incapacity. The final document needed in the basic estate plan would be a living will. The living will expresses an individual's desires for end-of-life care, or lack of it, so that these difficult and emotional decisions do not fall upon the family members.

SAMPLE ESTATE DESIGN

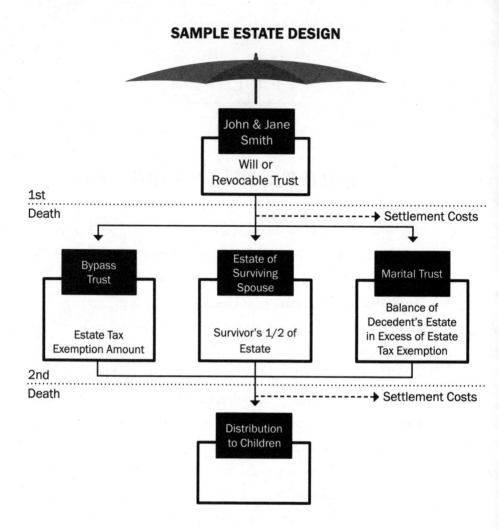

CHARITABLE PLANNING

Many believe that you must be philanthropic to benefit from a philanthropic legacy plan. However, we all are philanthropic whether we know it or not. If you are facing an estate tax problem, you need to decide whether to give your money to the charity that you choose or the one that Uncle Sam chooses. The default is already in place.

If you are wondering whether you should benefit your heirs or charity, it is important to understand that, in many cases, you can do both.

WAYS TO GIVE

The first step is to look at the ways someone could make a gift:

- outright gift
- charitable remainder trust
- charitable lead trust
- private foundation
- donor advised fund
- gift annuity

Those are just a few. A comprehensive review of charitable planning is beyond the scope of this book.

Many times, the way people gift depends on their charitable desires. Individuals active in a church or other charity may already be making donations before creating a legacy plan. Others may choose to delay charitable gifts until the future and even wait to contribute through the estate upon their death.

Even people who may not have a strong charitable desire still should consider the potential leverage for the estate that could enhance the transfers to heirs. For example, the charitable remainder trust can help reposition assets without paying capital gains taxes, create additional cash flow through charitable income tax deductions, or help to diversify assets to reduce risk.

Let's take a closer look at how a charitable remainder trust works:

1. The grantor (person who establishes the trust) contributes appreciated property or cash to the trustee (person who operates the trust) of the charitable remainder trust.

2. The grantor of the trust receives a charitable deduction based upon the fair market value of the remainder interest. The percentage of the remainder interest that can be taken as a charitable deduction in a particular year depends upon the status of the remainder beneficiary and the type of asset contributed to the trust. Any unused portion of the deduction can be carried forward for up to five years.

3. The charitable remainder trust pays income to an income beneficiary as designated by the grantor of the trust. The income beneficiary is often the grantor and his or her spouse. The term of the income can be for life or a set number of years.

4. At the end of the trust term, or after death, the assets remaining in the trust pass to the designated charity.

The charitable deduction creates cash flow by reducing taxable income for the years in which gifts are made (or deductions are carried forward). In addition, the deduction may reduce the grantor's effective income tax rate in any given year. Further, if the individual contributes appreciated property to the charitable remainder trust, the assets can be sold inside the trust without creating a taxable gain on the sale.

ASSETS TO CONSIDER GIFTING

It's not always easy to say which assets should be gifted. Most charities would prefer cash. However, if other assets in the estate have no sentimental value and there is no strong desire to transfer them to the next generation, those would make good choices to give to charity. In addition, life insurance may be a good asset to choose, as the value the charity would receive on death may be significantly higher than the value of the asset gifted.

TRANSFERRING ASSETS

A key component of most legacy plans will involve the gifting of assets during life from one generation to another. The issue centers on whether it is better to pass assets now or pass them at death through the estate.

ESTATE TAX LAWS

To address the timing of the asset transfers, we must first examine the impact of gift and estate tax laws. They must be examined together since they are intertwined in their impact. The federal estate tax exemption is a lifetime exemption. It can be used during life for eliminating gift tax or saved until death and the remaining amount will eliminate estate taxes. As of 2015, the exemption amount is $5.43 million per person. This exemption amount will grow since current law indexes this for inflation.

Any amount in the estate or gift that is in excess of the exemption amount will be subject to the estate or gift tax. As of 2015, the highest marginal federal estate tax rate is 40 percent.

PORTABILITY

A common estate planning tool for spouses is using both of their lifetime exemptions to offset the estate tax. One popular feature of the current estate tax law is "portability."

Here's how it works: If the first spouse to die doesn't use up his or her individual estate tax exemption, the surviving spouse can use what's left. That gives the couple a total exemption of twice the individual exemption amount. They can share that total exemption amount in the way that provides the greatest tax benefit.

To take advantage of the portability rule, an estate tax return must be filed when the first spouse dies, even if no tax will be due.

ANNUAL GIFT TAX EXCLUSION

In addition to the lifetime exemption, the tax code also provides for an annual gift tax exclusion. In 2015, the annual gift tax exclusion is $14,000 per donee. For example, if Mom wanted to make gifts to four children, the annual gift tax exclusion would equal $56,000 (4 x $14,000). The annual gift tax exclusion is also indexed for inflation. The annual gift tax exclusion is a "use it or lose it" provision. If it is not used by December 31 of each year, it is gone. This provision allows for smaller gifts to be made annually without having to use any of the lifetime exemption.

BASIS

A key issue to address prior to determining whether to make a gift now or hold the property until death is how the basis of the property will be treated.

If an asset is gifted, the basis in the property is transferred from the donor to the donee. Although the gift tax is determined at fair market value, this does not increase the basis in the property being gifted. Therefore, if there is an inherent gain in the property and the property is sold, the donee will now be responsible for paying the tax associated with the gain.

If an asset is passed through the estate at death, the basis of the property at the time of death is stepped up to equal the fair market value. In essence, all of the taxable gains in the assets of the estate are eliminated. The benefit of the stepped-up basis can be a great benefit to the heirs, especially for assets that have been depreciated prior to death.

VALUING THE GIFT: FAIR MARKET VALUE

When a gift is made, it is valued at its fair market value at the date of the gift for purposes of computing a gift tax liability. The definition of fair market value is the price at which the property would change hands between a willing buyer and a willing seller, neither being under any compulsion to buy or sell, and both having reasonable knowledge of the relevant facts.

Although the definition is simple, that might not be the case for many assets. Some assets may be difficult to value because they are rare and don't have a ready market. Business assets can be hard to value because an outside buyer may discount the value due to the company being closely held. However, the value must be determined in order to complete the gift.

When valuing a business, the value often is discounted because of lack of marketability or because the interest in question is not a controlling interest. On the contrary, a premium may be given to the value if the interest is a controlling interest.

Within the family context, these valuation discounts will allow for more assets to be given away while staying within the confines of the annual gift tax exclusion and lifetime exemption.

LIFE INSURANCE OVERVIEW

Most people think of life insurance as a poor place to invest money because of the low rate of return on their investment. Another concern is the notion that you have to die to receive the benefits. Many of the concerns are due to the lack of understanding of the tax benefits afforded to life insurance, the flexibility in design, and the other living benefits that can be received. To understand the flexibility and benefits of life insurance, we will begin with the basics.

The first question that many people raise is "How much does it cost?" When you ask what it costs, you're really asking, "What is the life insurance company going to charge for the mortality cost and their expenses to provide that particular policy?" That sets the line for the lower limit of the "premium amount." There is also a line that's called a modified endowment contract line, and that's the maximum amount of money that the tax code will allow to be paid into the policy before it's no longer treated as a life insurance policy but rather, during the holder's life, is treated more like an annuity.

Between these two lines is the amount of additional premium that you can put into a policy to build up cash value. That cash value is going to grow, tax deferred, and you can access it through withdrawals or loans on a tax-free basis. It's going to pay out a death benefit to beneficiaries on an income tax-free basis. If necessary, the life insurance policy can be structured to also pay out the death benefit estate tax-free.

Understanding Life Insurance – How Much Can I Put Into the Policy

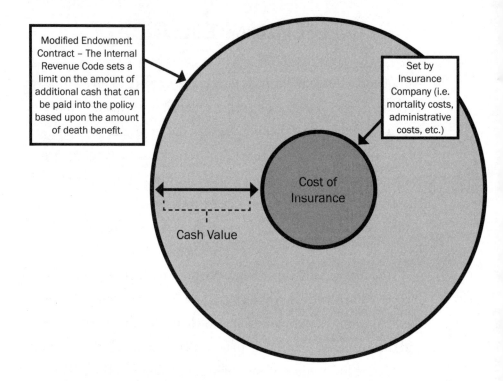

Modified Endowment Contract – The Internal Revenue Code sets a limit on the amount of additional cash that can be paid into the policy based upon the amount of death benefit.

Set by Insurance Company (i.e. mortality costs, administrative costs, etc.)

Cost of Insurance

Cash Value

The type of policy really determines the return on the cash value growth. You could purchase a term policy, which amounts to renting the insurance for a set period, perhaps 10, 20, or 30 years. If you die during that time, the beneficiary is paid, but typically, there is no cash value accumulation.

By contrast, permanent life insurance policies are typically designed to last beyond the life expectancies of most people. In addition, permanent policies may have the ability to accumulate cash value within the policy. Permanent insurance products are further divided into whole life or universal life policies.

Whole life has a fixed return based on the dividends paid by the company, which are based on the investment portfolio of the life insurance company.

Universal life policies include variable, fixed, and indexed products. With a variable policy, you basically are controlling the performance based on subaccounts or investments of the cash value. Fixed universal policies are similar to whole life in that the return is based on the portfolio of the company itself.

Indexed universal life is one of the newer types of policies. Indexed universal life is unique since the return of the policy will follow a set index, such as the S&P 500. These policies will, typically, have a floor and a cap on the gains attributed to the policy, based on the index return. The downside is protected by giving up some of the upside.

In other words, assume you have $100,000 in a policy with a floor of 0 percent and a cap of 12 percent. If the index in the first year went up 10 percent, your policy would be worth $110,000 excluding charges. If the market drops 30 percent in the second year, you would still have $110,000, thanks to the floor. You'll never have a negative year in the return.

In addition to the death benefit and the potential tax-free access to the cash values, life insurance can also provide benefits for chronic illness, critical illness, or long-term care. If your policy provides these types of benefits, you can access them to benefit your life while you are alive.

Life insurance is a tool, and within it are subtools. The type of policy you choose depends upon your goals and concerns.

BUY-SELL AGREEMENTS

A critical, yet often overlooked, component of many business plans is the implementation of a buy-sell agreement. A buy-sell agreement can be viewed as the business's prenuptial agreement. This is the agreement among the owners of the business on how they will transition the ownership of the business on the occurrence of certain triggers.

These triggers may include:

- Voluntary
    - Sale of ownership interest
    - Retire
- Involuntary
    - Death
    - Permanent disability
    - Bankruptcy
    - Divorce

A buy-sell agreement is also a bridge between the business and legacy planning for the business owners and their families. If properly structured and implemented, the buy-sell agreement can provide many advantages that will assist in reaching the owner's overall goals and objectives, as well as providing the succession of ownership.

In the absence of a buy-sell agreement, the ownership and control of the business may become an issue among competing parties, creating undue cost that could affect the viability of the business.

TYPES OF BUY-SELL AGREEMENTS

A buy-sell agreement is an agreement between two or more parties that states that upon the occurrence of a triggering event, one party has an obligation to buy the business interest from the party having the obligation to sell. There are three methods for structuring a buy-sell agreement: 1) a redemption agreement, 2) a cross-purchase agreement, and 3) a hybrid agreement. A general description is set forth as follows:

> **Redemption Agreement.** A redemption agreement is a contract between the business and the owners in which the owners agree to offer their interest in the business to the business upon the occurrence of a specified triggering event, on the terms and at the price set forth in the agreement.

REDEMPTION AGREEMENT

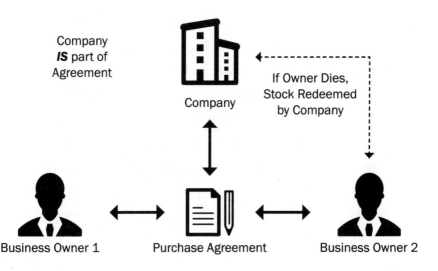

Company **IS** part of Agreement

Company

If Owner Dies, Stock Redeemed by Company

Business Owner 1   Purchase Agreement   Business Owner 2

Cross-Purchase Agreement. A cross-purchase agreement is a contract between or among the owners by which each partner agrees to offer his or her interest in the business for sale to the other owners upon the occurrence of a specified triggering event, on the terms and at the price set forth in the agreement.

CROSS-PURCHASE AGREEMENT

Company
IS NOT part of
Agreement

Company

Business Owner 1   Purchase Agreement   Business Owner 2

Hybrid Agreement. A hybrid agreement is a contract between the business and the business owners and also between or among the owners. Depending upon the structure of the agreement, the partner's interest will either be redeemed by the business or purchased by the other owners upon the occurrence of a specified triggering event, on the terms and at the price set forth in the agreement. The agreement will state which party will have the first option to purchase, and if the option isn't exercised, then the remaining party will have a mandatory obligation to purchase the interest.

The hybrid agreement has the advantage of giving the surviving owner the choice to determine what will be the best option for making the purchase. The effect on the selling owner will be the same.

HYBRID AGREEMENT

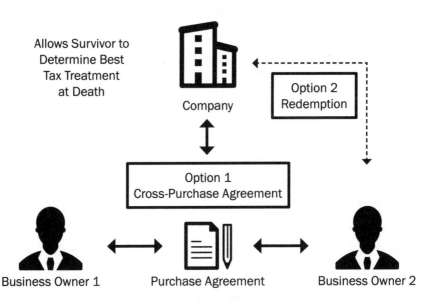

Allows Survivor to Determine Best Tax Treatment at Death

Company

Option 2 Redemption

Option 1 Cross-Purchase Agreement

Business Owner 1   Purchase Agreement   Business Owner 2

BENEFITS OF A BUY-SELL AGREEMENT

The first, and often most important, advantage of a buy-sell agreement is that it can prevent the sale or other transfer of ownership interests outside the current ownership structure. A second benefit of a buy-sell agreement is that it creates a ready market for each owner's interest in the business, easing the liquidity problems created by the ownership of a block of closely held ownership interest at the owner's death. A third benefit of a buy-sell agreement is that the agreement can help establish the value of the business. While not all agreements will accomplish this goal, a carefully drafted buy-sell agreement can dispense with or facilitate the difficulties involved in valuing a business for tax purposes. A buy-sell agreement should set out the method of setting the purchase price. The purchase price can be a set amount that is adjusted annually, or it can be a formula or an appraisal.

FUNDING THE BUY-SELL AGREEMENT

Finding the cash to purchase the ownership interest of a retired, disabled, or deceased owner can be a major problem for a closely held business and the surviving owners. To alleviate the concerns set forth above, the buy-sell agreement can be funded with life and disability insurance. Life insurance is often the preferred means of funding the testamentary purchases under a buy-sell agreement, because the death benefit is financed by a series of smaller premium payments, and the proceeds are received by the beneficiary free of income tax.

Another advantage of using cash value life insurance is that the cash value can also be used to buy out the interest of a partner for events other than death. This will help to reduce the burden on the partner continuing to operate the business, while still providing the departing partner some or all of the purchase price.

Disability insurance is an excellent tool to fund the purchase of an ownership interest that is being sold pursuant to the owner's permanent disability. The disability insurance can be purchased to provide a lump sum payment or a series of payments.

CAPTIVE INSURANCE COMPANIES

Captive insurance companies are a unique planning tool that can be utilized by many profitable companies that currently have uninsured risks that may affect their business operations. A captive is a small insurance company that is owned by one or more business owners to provide insurance for the business. It is a legally licensed, limited-purpose property and casualty insurer.

To be clear, a captive is an insurance company, not an insurance product. It insures the business risk of the owner's operating company. The captive can issue policies, collect premiums, establish reserves, and pay claims.

The captive can be owned by the owners of the operating company. In addition, the owners of the business can take the additional steps to incorporate the ownership of the captive into their legacy plans.

The key benefits of a captive include a tax deduction to the operating company of up to $1.2 million per year for property and casualty insurance premiums, which is specifically permitted by the Internal Revenue Code under Section 831(b). The tax code permits the captive to receive insurance premiums, which are tax deductible to the operating business. This means that the business paying the premiums will deduct up to $1.2 million per year for insurance costs, but that amount is not taxable to the captive.

The captive does not pay tax on premiums received but does pay tax on all investment income generated by the captive at normal corporate rates. When a captive is sold or liquidated, the owners will pay tax on the gain at long-term capital gains rates.

A captive's main business purpose is to insure the risks of its owners or the companies affiliated with its owners. Captives can be formed by any type of business: financial institutions, manufacturers, retailers, construction companies, and service businesses, to name only a few. A captive can provide virtually any type of insurance, as long as the laws of the state or country in which it is domiciled (i.e., incorporated, licensed, managed, and operated) allow the line of business to be underwritten.

MANAGING THE RISKS

Managing risk is a key element for any successful business. Poor risk management has led to the failure of many business ventures. Many of the risks are easy to identify because business owners can buy commercial insurance policies to cover these risks: automobile, malpractice, general liability, workers compensation, and so on. However, there are other risks that the business owner may be unaware of or may choose to ignore as simply "the cost of doing business." Many business owners may choose to take on these additional risks and self-insure due to the fact that the risks are either hard to identify or the business owner cannot purchase insurance at a cost-effective price.

The captive can help solve this issue. Many types of risk could be insured by a captive, as identified and quantified by an actuary. Some of those risks may include:

- deductibles

- exclusions

- business interruption

- independent contractor risk

- warranty

- product liability

- administrative action or investigation

- fines and penalties

- litigation or dispute resolution

The risk must be real. The risk has to be identifiable to the business and quantifiable by an independent actuary. The captive is regulated and subject to the rules of the jurisdiction in which it is formed. In addition, the captive must satisfy the rules set out in the Internal Revenue Code and regulations.

WHY USE A CAPTIVE?

The primary purpose of implementing a captive is to save money on the cost of insurance.

First, by underwriting the insurance needs of the business, the captive can capture and retain the underwriting profits that would ordinarily be lost to a commercial carrier. Additionally, considering that commercial carriers have costs that must be priced into their policies, such as the expense of compensating agents, marketing and advertising expenses, executive compensation, and so on, there is a great deal of added expense that can be saved through the use of a captive.

Second, even where the business decides to keep commercial insurance in place against particular risks, the captive can be used to reduce costs by raising deductibles, lowering coverage limits, or increasing exclusions—the idea being for the business to find the point where the commercial insurance is most economical, and then use the captive to insure around that area.

POLICIES

The captive will issue an insurance policy to the operating company outlining the risks being covered and the coverage period. This is important since the captive must operate as an insurer or reinsurer in the domicile in which it is formed.

After the coverage period, any underwriting profits not paid out in claims can be used or distributed by the captive. If the captive retains the funds, then it will continue to pay taxes on any additional investment gains. If the captive chooses to distribute some of the underwriting profits to the shareholders, then the shareholders will pay long-term capital gains on the dividend. At the time the captive is terminated, the shareholders will pay long-term capital gains on the liquidating distribution from the captive.

RISK SHARING

The tax code and regulations related to captive insurance companies hold that captives cannot be just a dollar-for-dollar self-insurance program. There must be an element of risk sharing. The regulations set out safe harbors to provide guidance in this area.

Safe Harbor #1: More than 50 percent of the company's risk exposure must be derived from insuring third parties.

CAPTIVE INSURANCE COMPANY — POOLED RISK

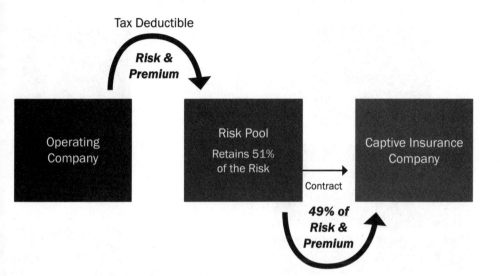

Safe Harbor #2: The next safe harbor addresses brother/sister companies. If a captive insurance company is completely owned by a holding company, this holding company also owns 100 percent of at least 12 affiliated companies.

CAPTIVE INSURANCE COMPANY —
BROTHER/SISTER COMPANIES

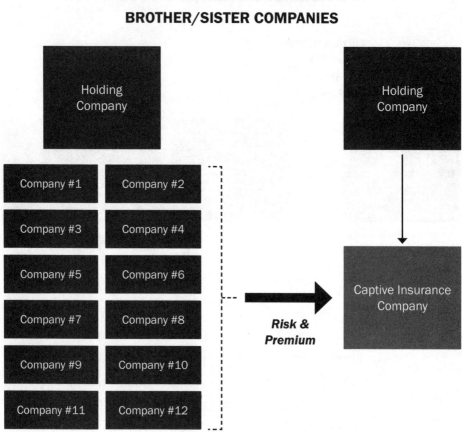

Safe Harbor #3: A group captive structure that can meet the risk sharing required by the tax code is also allowed. In this type of structure, a group of unrelated and independent entities each form their own wholly owned captive insurance company, and each captive directly insures the risks of its affiliated owner. In order to provide adequate risk shifting and distribution, the unrelated captives subsequently purchase reinsurance policies from the other captives in the pooled structure.

CAPTIVE REINSURANCE COMPANY

Another way to account for the risk sharing requirements is by utilizing an affiliated reinsurance company. In this type of structure, the premium would be paid to a true frontline insurance company. This insurance company would be unrelated to the operating company or its owners. The insurance company would keep some of the premiums and risk and reinsure the remaining risk to a captive reinsurance company owned by the owners of the operating company.

CAPTIVE REINSURANCE COMPANY

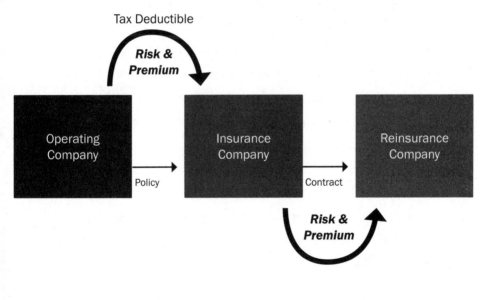

BUSINESS ENTITIES

A key component of many estates is the operating businesses and asset holding entities. This is an area that can create an opportunity for planning or a headache. The issues inherent in this area of the planning process revolve around the type of entity structure, control of the business, and how this asset is transferred to the appropriate heir.

Selection of the appropriate business form is a complicated process involving numerous alternatives, variables, and preferences. Variables to consider include tax considerations, liability exposure, ease of formation, management structure, and succession of ownership. Choosing the appropriate entity includes analyzing the various alternatives and prioritizing these alternatives. This process of selecting the proper entity form requires a balancing of business law and tax objectives, as well as individual preferences and goals.

Choosing the right business entity is more important than ever before due to the expansion of entity choices. The variety of entity choices include:

- sole proprietorships
- general partnerships
- C corporations
- S corporations
- limited liability companies (multiple-member and single-member)

- limited partnerships

- limited liability partnerships

TAX CONSIDERATIONS

One of the basic considerations when choosing an entity is the effect of federal taxation. The Internal Revenue Code effectively divides entities into two categories, "taxable" and "pass-through" entities. In a pass-through entity, the owners of the entity are responsible for the tax on their share of the entity's income, gain, deductions, and credits, whether or not any money or property is actually distributed to the owners. Pass-through entities include general partnerships, limited partnerships, S corporations, limited liability partnerships, and qualifying LLCs.

In taxable entities, the entity pays an income tax on earnings before distributing such earnings to its owners. Since the entity is responsible for paying the tax on its earnings, distributions to the owners are made out of post-tax income. Therefore, the income of a taxable entity is taxed at both the entity level and the individual level. The most familiar taxable entity is the C corporation.

A third category has now emerged: disregarded entities. A disregarded entity is an entity that is disregarded for income tax filing. A single-member LLC that does not elect to be treated as a corporation will be "disregarded as an entity separate from its owner." The activities of a disregarded single-member LLC are treated "in the same manner as a sole proprietorship." Therefore, if a single-member LLC is owned by a corporation, the single-member LLCs assets are treated as an unincorporated division owned directly by the corporation for federal tax purposes.

MANAGEMENT

An integral part of the choice of entity process is organizing the management structure of the new entity. Critical decision points include 1) retained control by the owner, 2) consolidation of control in one or more persons, and 3) flexibility in structuring and changing management.

The simplest form of management is a sole proprietorship. In a sole proprietorship, the owner is allowed full control of the business entity without the need and/or responsibility to obtain consent from other parties. The opposite side of this spectrum is the corporation. A corporation is designed to separate ownership in the shareholders, with management duties divided between the board of directors and the officers of the corporation. Each party has distinct roles, with shareholders electing the board of directors, directors electing the officers and giving them the overall guidance for the entity, and the officers operating the day-to-day operations of the entity. The limited partnership contains a similar element of flexibility to the sole proprietorship if there is a single general partner. However, due to the inherent nature of a limited partner, the limited partners are offered few, if any, management duties.

Historically, the choice for the management structure was limited due to the simple fact that if ownership and control were combined, potential liability exposure followed. If a corporate structure was used, flexibility was limited. Therefore, the drafters of LLC legislation sought to combine the flexibility in management of a partnership with the liability protection of a corporation. Thus, the revolution in the choice of entity arena began. The first step in analyzing the management structure is determining how much individual control the owners desire, and second, the liability protection needed.

SUCCESSION OF OWNERSHIP

A primary consideration when structuring any closely held business involves determining succession of ownership of the business. Such planning is necessary in order to create an effective exit strategy for the owners. Discussions in this area must involve both the state law criteria as well as the tax consequences.

Most succession of ownership issues can be resolved if identified properly. Preparation of a buy-sell agreement, along with proper funding, will allow the business owners to easily pass the business to succeeding owners either within or outside the family. Proper planning will provide owners with the appropriate exit strategy and assist in the overall business and legacy plan.

ASSET PROTECTION

Liability exposure is another pivotal element to be determined by the business owner. Historically, the choices were 1) a sole proprietor with liability exposure for all of the liabilities generated from the venture, 2) a general partnership with the partners jointly and severally liable for the obligations of the partnership, 3) a limited partnership in which at least one general partner is liable for the debts of the partnership, and 4) a corporation that shielded its owners from liability but with cumbersome rules to operate under.

The current trend has been to create entities that provide liability protection, while allowing for pass-through tax treatment and flexibility in management (i.e., LLCs and limited liability partnerships). The rationale for use of these forms is to provide an alternative to the corporate form of limited liability for owners while providing flexibility in management. The liability exposure that principles of an entity should be concerned with includes liability for personal conduct as well as for conduct of other principals, employees, and agents. These liabilities may be satisfied out of the assets of the entity and to the extent the entity has insufficient assets to satisfy all claims, from the assets of the principals.

With the current entity choices available, liability exposure should be minimized in most situations without giving up favorable tax benefits and entity structure. However, if proper planning isn't employed, the unwary owner may sacrifice one or all of these elements.

USE IN THE PLANNING PROCESS

Limited partnerships and limited liability companies taxed as partnerships are especially attractive in the family setting, providing a vehicle to pass on family wealth as well as to hold family business assets. In addition, these entities provide an effective method to reduce the value of gifted interests.

PARTNERSHIP TAXATION

A primary motive for selecting a limited partnership or limited liability company taxed as a partnership is to obtain the preferential treatment of pass-through taxation. In addition, partnership taxation provides other tax advantages. Some of the more important tax advantages are discussed below.

Generally, neither the partnership nor the individual partners will recognize gain or loss upon the formation of a partnership. However, there are several exceptions to this general rule. First, a partner will recognize gain if the partner contributes to the partnership property in which liabilities exceed the adjusted basis of the partner's partnership interest. Second, if a partner receives an interest in the partnership due to services rendered, the partner will recognize income equal to the value of the services rendered.

Third, if a partner transfers to a partnership property that would be considered an investment company, gain may be recognized.

BASIS

Upon the contribution of property to the partnership, the partnership will generally receive a basis equal to the adjusted basis of the property in the hands of the contributing partner, and the contributing partner will take a basis, in the partnership, equal to the adjusted basis of the property contributed. Furthermore, under partnership taxation, each partner's basis is increased by the partner's share of the partnership's liabilities. The amount of liabilities allocated to each partner depends on whether the liability is characterized as a recourse or nonrecourse liability. The allocation of recourse debt among the partners is designed to allocate the debt to the partner who will bear the ultimate economic risk of loss.

SPECIAL ALLOCATION

One of the most attractive features of partnership taxation is the potential to create special ownership interests ("special allocations") in a partnership's capital and profits. Special allocations refer to any allocations that are different from a partner's interest in the partnership. A partnership is not a taxpaying entity but only a vehicle for determining the taxable income, gain, loss, deduction, or credit of a joint operation in which two or more partners participate. Therefore, a provision in the partnership agreement is necessary to allocate those items, determined at the partnership level, among the partners, for tax purposes.

Special allocations are governed by Internal Revenue Code section 704(b). The thrust of this section is to ensure that a partner's distributive share of partnership tax items conforms to the partner's share of the economic consequences of those items. Within this limitation, the partners may, by agreement, use any allocation that they choose.

INCOME TAX PLANNING

A limited partnership or a limited liability company provides excellent structures when implementing a comprehensive income tax reduction plan. Both entities allow extensive planning to be performed, while a significant amount of control can still be maintained.

In organizing a comprehensive income tax plan, the ultimate goal must be identified. The ultimate goal in this section is to reduce overall income taxes to the family without losing control of the assets. This goal of reducing income taxes is realized by shifting family income from the parent's typically higher marginal income tax bracket to the children's or grandchildren's lower marginal income tax bracket. If this is accomplished, the overall "family" income taxes paid will be decreased.

There are two different alternatives that can be employed to achieve this goal. The first and easiest method is through a gifting program in which gifts are made annually by the parents to the children or grandchildren, utilizing the annual gift tax exclusion or lifetime exemption. As gifts are made, the income that would have been reported on the parent's income tax return is now reported on the children's or grandchildren's income tax returns at a potentially lower marginal income tax rate.

The second and more complicated method of lowering the family's overall income taxes is through the use of special allocations. In many instances, the children or grandchildren are not in a position to utilize specific tax items, such as losses, depreciation, or amortization expenses. Therefore, if the partnership is properly organized and operated, the partners can allocate these specific items to the parents, thus allowing these items to be utilized on the parent's individual income tax return to offset other income.

Finally, partnership taxation allows for flexibility in organizing future acquisitions by allowing assets to be either contributed to, or distributed from, the partnership, without triggering capital gain recognition. This flexibility allows for future income tax planning as the overall needs of the family change.

FAMILY OFFICE

A great opportunity exists when the legacy planning is combined with the business planning if a family office is created. In many situations, Mom and Dad have built up a successful business over time, and by the time the children or grandchildren enter the business, the key decisions that allowed the business to grow were made years before. Therefore, the children and grandchildren may not understand why certain decisions were or were not made.

Including family members in ownership of the business creates the opportunity to operate a family office within the family. In this setting, Mom and Dad can now shift the "business talk" from the kitchen table to the board room. This will allow them to take on their roles as business executives and educate the family on not only how and why business decisions are made but also on how to continue the legacy that has been created and is being passed on to future generations.

We all received instructions on how to drive a car before we were issued our driver's license. Why not incorporate this same concept into the estate and business planning process? We can create a situation in which the future executives of the company can be trained to take the business to the next level when their time arrives.

DYNASTY TRUSTS

Wealth accumulation requires time, sacrifice, and perseverance—and once you have wealth, it can be a challenge to keep it and pass it on to serve your family well for generations. Heirs often lose much of what they inherit. That can happen intentionally or unintentionally, due to excessive spending habits, divorce settlements, claims of creditors, or poor investment choices.

Taxes, too, are a major threat that can erode your wealth. Unfortunately, wealth is not easily transferred from one generation to the next. Inadequate planning can allow a variety of taxes to take the majority of your estate. Federal estate taxes can reach 40 percent. In addition, many states have enacted estate taxes that can take as much as 20 percent of your estate as well. Retirement funds are subject to both income and estate taxes. Additionally, gifts you make to your grandchildren can be further eroded by the additional "generation-skipping" tax. Fortunately, these taxes can be reduced or entirely eliminated with the proper planning.

Our current tax laws are designed to impede the passing of wealth from one generation to the next. To make sure property is taxed at each generation, the law imposes a 40 percent generation-skipping transfer tax (GST tax). The GST tax applies to transfer of property to a person two or more generations younger than the person making the transfer. This would apply, for example, to transfers from a grandparent to a grandchild. Note that the GST tax is in addition to the gift tax and estate tax. Together, these taxes are commonly referred to as transfer taxes.

A solution to this problem is the dynasty trust. It accomplishes two key goals. First, it eliminates transfer taxes to future generations. Assets held in a dynasty trust can benefit your descendants without being subject to tax in their respective estates. Second, a dynasty trust eliminates the risks associated with the heirs, such as divorce or creditor claims.

A dynasty trust can hold property in trust perpetually, without the further imposition of any estate, gift, or other transfer tax liability.

On the other hand, income taxes, with respect to the income generated by the trust, would usually be paid in the same manner as any other income generated by an irrevocable trust. Thus, the trust may be established as an independent taxpaying entity. Alternatively, the trust may be structured as an income-tax defective grantor trust while the grantor of the trust is living. It still permits the grantor to avail himself of various estate, gift, and GST tax savings.

In a nutshell, dynasty trusts are multigenerational trusts that can be designed to provide distributions to your descendants and heirs. While the trust may be designed to be perpetual in nature, it can also be designed to continue for only a set number of generations.

DYNASTY TRUST AND LIFE INSURANCE

Life insurance can be an excellent asset inside a dynasty trust to provide leverage to the legacy passing to future generations. The amount of the exemption used when seeding the trust is the amount to pay the premiums. However, the amount to the heirs is the death benefit. Again, we see the tax being allocated to the seed but the heirs enjoying the harvest.

With the growing popularity of survivorship, or second-to-die, life insurance, this type of policy could further enhance the leverage of the gift over the premiums paid by the trust.

RULES AGAINST PERPETUITIES

In many states, there are certain restrictions on how long property may be held in trust. These concepts are founded in the common law and now, with a number of exceptions, have been incorporated into the statutory provisions of these states. The general concept of this "rule against perpetuities" was to prohibit a grantor, whether by a gift during his lifetime or by a devise at his death, from controlling the disposition of property from the grave. There was a public policy concern that real property might have restrictions against its use forever, thus limiting the potential growth and development of an economic center. Accordingly, in one form or another, many states have restrictions on the right of an owner to sell, devise, or donate property for a period longer than 21 years after the death of certain people who are living at the creation of the transfer restriction.

Some states have developed a rule similar to the rule against perpetuities and known as the "power of suspension of alienation," which also restricts the length of time that property may be controlled beyond the transfer by the original owner. Many states have abolished the rule against perpetuities, or they limit the reach of the rule to only transfers of interests in real property. These statutes, in essence, recognize that there is no public policy justification for limiting the term of a trust or other transfer mechanism that restricts the disposition of personal property only. In order to establish a true dynasty trust, it is necessary to establish a trust in one of these states or to establish a connection with a state that would allow the continuance of the trust on a multigenerational or perpetual basis.

GENERATION-SKIPPING TRANSFER TAX

Congress, seeing that many wealthy families implemented long-term trusts so that the estate tax could be avoided for several generations, adopted the generation-skipping transfer tax (GST). The GST tax is imposed at the highest marginal estate tax rate—currently 40 percent—on generation-skipping transfers. The GST tax is separate from, and in addition to, the gift and estate taxes.

Internal Revenue Code §2632(a) provides an exemption from the GST tax in the amount of $5 million per individual, indexed for inflation. If the dynasty trust were to be funded with property on which the grantor and the grantor's spouse maximize their GST tax exemption, which, as of 2015, is $10.86 million in the aggregate, substantial value could be contributed to the trust. Once exempted from the GST tax, the contributions to the trust, as well as appreciation and accumulated income on the property, will thenceforth remain beyond the reach of federal transfer taxation so long as the property remains in the dynasty trust.

BENEFITS PROVIDED TO THE BENEFICIARIES

A variety of benefits can be provided to the beneficiaries of a dynasty trust. It is up to the grantor to determine the type of benefits to provide. Additionally, the grantor needs to determine whether benefits flow to primary beneficiaries, to secondary beneficiaries, or to both.

A common design technique for distributing assets to beneficiaries of the trust involves designating beneficiaries as primary or secondary beneficiaries. Secondary beneficiaries are generally defined as descendants of primary beneficiaries. For example, assume that a grantor has three children, each of whom has children of his or her own. The dynasty trust can be divided into three shares, one for each child of the grantor. Each child will be the primary beneficiary of his or her share of the dynasty trust. He or she will receive the benefits designated for a primary beneficiary.

The grantor could also provide benefits for secondary beneficiaries or the descendants. Generally, benefits for secondary beneficiaries are less generous than those provided to primary beneficiaries. The benefits to be provided to each type of beneficiary must be decided by the grantor. These benefits could be conservative (for example, benefits solely for the education of the beneficiaries) or liberal (a complete distribution of trust assets to the beneficiaries). In between are various degrees of benefits, such as:

- education, limited to a four-year college degree

- education of any type beneficial to the beneficiary

- emergency medical needs

- all medical and health-care needs

- payment of basic needs and support of a beneficiary unable to otherwise support himself or herself

- seed money to start a business or profession

- seed money to purchase real estate

- distribution of specified amounts or percentages of trust assets upon attainment of predetermined ages of a beneficiary

- outright distribution of trust assets upon the occurrence of a specified event or the attainment of a specified age

The grantor must determine how generously trust benefits will be distributed to the beneficiaries. The type of assets used to fund the dynasty trust will have some bearing on those decisions. For example, active business interests will normally be distributed more quickly than passive investments, such as a stock portfolio.

DESIGN

A dynasty trust should be irrevocable so that it cannot be altered by the grantors of the trust or by succeeding generations of beneficiaries in a manner that would subject all or a portion of the assets in the trust to transfer tax liability, regardless of whether that liability is a gift or an estate tax liability. Generally, with the formation of an irrevocable trust, there is no intention that the individual grantor who established the trust will ever receive any benefit from the trust. Instead, the focus is on the establishment of a trust that will provide a basis for estate tax savings. Making the trust irrevocable helps to ensure that the beneficiaries will not be able to alter the trust in any manner that could cause ownership of trust assets to pass to the beneficiaries, since that could negate the planned transfer tax savings.

This does not mean, however, that substantial benefits of the trust may not be made available to the beneficiaries of the trust. The trustee can be given broad discretion to distribute the income and the principal of the trust for one or more beneficiaries for reasons originally enumerated by the grantors upon the establishment of the trust. Trustees may also be given significant flexibility in establishing subtrusts within the trust to accommodate other special needs for assets held by the trust.

TRUSTEE APPOINTMENT, SUCCESSION, AND REMOVAL

A dynasty trust may last for several generations. Trustee provisions must be designed to take into account this longevity. The initial trustee for the dynasty trust may be a person or an institution. A trust company is a logical choice for administering a dynasty trust due to the length of time the trust will be in existence.

The trust needs to have flexible provisions regarding the appointment of additional successor trustees or the removal of a trustee. If trustees become unable to serve in that capacity, successor trustees will need to be appointed. If all successor trustees initially selected by the grantor are no longer available to serve as trustees, then the trust document should have a mechanical approach to selecting a new trustee. For example, the then-current beneficiaries of the trust (or their legal representative) should be able to select a new trustee.

The beneficiaries, or a trust protector, should also have power to remove a trustee who is not fulfilling his or her fiduciary responsibilities. For example, if a trustee refuses to make distributions that are appropriate under the trust document, or if the trustee is making imprudent investment choices, the trust protector or trust beneficiaries (or their legal representatives) should be able to remove the trustee.

A cotrustee can also create a good balance in the trust administration. For instance, a trust company could be designated as a cotrustee along with a family member. The trust company would provide the professional management while the family trustee would provide more of the personal touch to the trust.

SPECIAL PROVISIONS

Since the dynasty trust will, presumably, be an irrevocable trust, it is important that thoughtful drafting go into its formation:

> *Pot trust vs. split-up.* Perhaps the single most important issue is whether the trust should be one single conglomeration of assets (a pot trust) or whether there should be divisions of the trust in each generation to establish separate trusts. A pot trust is a single trust pursuant to which the trustee will make distributions to individuals at various generational levels. The trust is not split up, such as along family lines. This provides for easier management and facilitates economies of scale due to the considerable size of the "pot." Conversely, the trust may be split up along family lines. This would encourage additions of property by the original grantors' descendants since those descendants will more likely contribute to the wealth of their own offspring than to the wealth of more remote relatives.
>
> *Withdrawal rights and powers of distribution.* Presumably, the trust would be established to provide that principal, and income may be available to the descendants and at the sole discretion of the trustee. One may also consider whether superiority withdrawal powers should be established in each generation. For example, the grantor-parents may decide, during the lives of their children, that the trust is to be divided into one share for each surviving child and that each child is to be a sole beneficiary of a separate trust within the dynasty trust. The grantors should also determine

whether they would allow some distributions for the benefit of their children's descendants during their lifetimes. If a separate trust format were selected, each trust would be divided again at each generation to the extent that there were survivors within that family line. The trust may provide that if there were no survivors within the family lines, the assets could be distributed and continue to be held by the other segregated trusts within that dynasty trust.

Access to assets. To provide long-term flexibility, the grantors may also want to provide additional flexibility for succeeding generations to access and direct the disposition of the assets. One concept that appears to be compelling is the use of a special power of appointment, designed so that the exercise of the special power of appointment would not cause the inclusion of the assets in the estate of the holder of the power. However, the wisdom of using such a power for a long-term trust may frustrate the ultimate purpose of the trust if the power is exercised in a manner that postpones or suspends the vesting and absolute ownership of the property.

On the other hand, the granting of a power that would allow a primary beneficiary of each subtrust to withdraw up to 5 percent or $5,000 of each trust during a year may have significant appeal so that the grantors can assure that the assets will not be maintained for the benefit of the trustees but rather for the benefit of the beneficiaries.

Broad trustee powers. Perhaps the most important aspect of drafting the dynasty trust is to give the trustees broad power to terminate or amend the trust and to establish subtrusts as legal and tax consequences change. The trustee and/or trust protector should be given the power to terminate or amend the trust if its perpetuation would be unduly burdensome or unwise. Termination or amendment could also be authorized if tax or other legislative changes make the continuation of the trust inadvisable from a tax perspective or frustrate the original purpose of the grantors. As pointed out below, it may also be wise to permit the trustee to move the trust from jurisdiction to jurisdiction based on the wisdom of how property should be managed and how the income from a trust is taxed at a particular time.

Trust protector. Due to the longevity of the dynasty trust, it is prudent to appoint a trust protector. The trust protector serves as the last line of defense against defective administration. The trust protector is given power to discharge a trustee if that trustee is not fulfilling fiduciary responsibilities or is not adhering to the provisions of the trust instrument. The trust protector may be an individual or a committee. It is advisable to start with a single individual but also to provide in the trust instrument for the appointment of either additional individuals to serve in that capacity or a committee of individuals, such as family members.

INCOME AND TRANSFER TAX ISSUES

The dynasty trust should, in all events, be designed in a manner to avoid the imposition of additional estate, gift, or generation-skipping taxes upon the grantors or beneficiaries of the trust.

To draft otherwise would be to negate the benefits of the dynasty trust and the very concept of preserving the assets from the transfer tax system. On the other hand, from a less positive perspective, the income taxes that are imposed upon trusts are significant and in most cases, would subject the income of the trust to substantial federal and state income tax on the income earned. If the income is not required to be distributed, it would appear to make sense to retain the income in the trust even though there may be income taxes imposed on the income.

On the other hand, it may be wise to consider establishing the dynasty trust in a jurisdiction where at least the state income tax obligations may be avoided. Alternatively, the trustees could adopt a philosophy of investing in nonincome-producing assets and long-term investments, which would benefit the successive generations. The trustees could also consider purchasing assets that could be made available for use by the beneficiaries. Under present case law (2015), there does not appear to be any income, gift, estate, or GST-tax consequence for permitting the beneficiaries of the trust to use trust property. The trustees could also consider making investments in assets that would not provide trust accounting income during periods when the beneficiaries of a particular trust were not desirous of receiving any distributions.

CREDITOR PROTECTION

Several methods can be used in the design of the dynasty trust to ensure that some creditor protection is provided to the beneficiaries and perhaps, for the trust assets. For a domestic-based trust, the grantor would normally consider using a spendthrift clause that allows the withholding of distributions from a beneficiary to protect the beneficiary from making distributions to beneficiaries' creditors or an estranged spouse who might be seeking alimony or support upon the dissolution of a marriage. Employing the spendthrift clause in the traditional sense provides the individual, at a minimum, with a method of discouraging potential creditors from attacking the distributions of the trust assets.

PERPETUAL VALUES TRUST

The majority of trust agreements focus on the legal and tax provisions. Although these provisions are important to achieving the desired outcome, many trusts ignore the "legacy" that can be achieved by outlining the do's and don'ts that reflect the values of the grantors of the trust.

The incentives or disincentives are the part of the trust that can encourage or discourage the behavior of the beneficiaries of the trust for generations. In order to receive income and/or principal, the beneficiary would have to meet the terms of the trust to the satisfaction of the trustee.

The tax and legal provisions of the trust provide the structure to pass the estate from the grantors of the trust to succeeding generations with the least amount of tax erosion. But the incentives and disincentives are the provisions that pass on the attributes of the trust's grantors.

When establishing the incentives and disincentives in the trust, the key question to ask is what is important to the grantors of the trust. What type of lifestyle do the grantors want to encourage or discourage for future generations? As many have seen, left unchecked, the trust funds can be squandered in ways not intended. But with careful planning, the trust funds can be used to supplement future generations. Based upon the client's desires, the incentives can be made to affect only the trust income or only the principal or both income and principal.

Some of these incentives may include:

- supplemental income, which may provide a percentage match to money earned or an additional amount to bring the beneficiaries to a certain standard of living

- money to buy a home, which could be the down payment or the entire purchase price

- money for education, which could include any level of education as determined by the grantors

- money to start or purchase a business

- money for charitable work

Some of the disincentives may include:

- withholding money if the beneficiary is incarcerated

- withholding money for education if the beneficiary is not obtaining adequate grades or on track to graduate

- withholding money if the beneficiary is abusing drugs, alcohol, and so on

With the criteria in place, the trustee now has direction on how to utilize the trust funds. The grantor may also want to consider giving the trustee or trust protector the power to make additions or deletions to this list of incentives or disincentives to further meet the grantor's vision of how this legacy should come to fruition.